SERVANTS OF THE DEVIL

The Facilitators of the Criminal and Terrorist Networks

Editors

Norman Bailey
The Institute of World Politics, Washington DC, USA

Bernard Touboul
Taccit, UK

World Scientific

NEW JERSEY · LONDON · SINGAPORE · BEIJING · SHANGHAI · HONG KONG · TAIPEI · CHENNAI · TOKYO

Published by

World Scientific Publishing Co. Pte. Ltd.
5 Toh Tuck Link, Singapore 596224
USA office: 27 Warren Street, Suite 401-402, Hackensack, NJ 07601
UK office: 57 Shelton Street, Covent Garden, London WC2H 9HE

Library of Congress Cataloging-in-Publication Data
Names: Bailey, Norman A., editor. | Touboul, Bernard, editor.
Title: Servants of the devil : the facilitators of the criminal and
    terrorist networks / editors, Norman Bailey, The Institute of World Politics,
    Washington, DC, USA, Bernard Touboul, TACCIT Ltd, Great Britain.
Description: New Jersey : World Scientific, [2021] | Includes
    bibliographical references.
Identifiers: LCCN 2020047425 | ISBN 9789811229121 (hardcover) | ISBN
    9789811229138 (ebook) | ISBN 9789811229145 (ebook other)
Subjects: LCSH: Terrorism--Economic aspects. | International crimes.
Classification: LCC HV6431 .S4598 2021 | DDC 363.325--dc23
LC record available at https://lccn.loc.gov/2020047425

British Library Cataloguing-in-Publication Data
A catalogue record for this book is available from the British Library.

For any available supplementary material, please visit
https://www.worldscientific.com/worldscibooks/10.1142/12067#t=suppl

Desk Editors: Balasubramanian Shanmugam/Karimah Samsudin

Typeset by Stallion Press
Email: enquiries@stallionpress.com

This book is dedicated to all victims, abused, enslaved, exploited, or murdered by criminal syndicates and terrorist organizations, which have been allowed to deeply penetrate our lives, due to the lack of public consciousness as well as good governance.

About the Editors

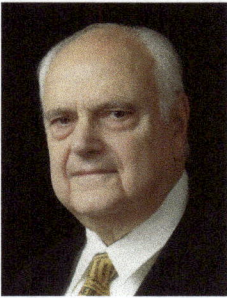

Norman A. Bailey, Ph.D., is Professor of Economic Statecraft at the Institute of World Politics, Washington, DC. His background includes experience in the armed forces, business, finance, academia, and consulting. He has served on the staff of the National Security Council and the Office of the Director of National Intelligence in Washington. He is the author, co-author, or editor of five books, three monographs, and hundreds of articles.

Bernard Touboul is an International Expert in Customs Administration and Enforcement, Border Management, and International Trade Facilitation. He has an extensive experience as a consultant in institutional development in many countries in the world. He was an official of the French Customs Service and holds graduate degrees in International Trade, Business Administration, and Political Sciences specialized in national security.

About the Authors

Rachel Ehrenfeld, Ph.D., is Founder and President of New York-based American Center for Democracy and The Economic Warfare Institute. She publishes, lectures, and consults widely for public and private entities. She initiated legislation in New York state on anti-libel tourism, referred to as "Rachel's Law" and the "Speech Act".

Yitzhak Zahavy is Head of Compliance at Jerusalem Venture Partners, co-founder of Taxlucent, and a management consultant. He was previously with Price Waterhouse, Goldman Sachs, and Credit Suisse. He holds the degree of MBA and has lectured widely.

Yaron Hazan is currently with Thetaray, AI solutions provider for anti-money laundering, anti-fraud, and cyber-detection for banks and regulators. He was formerly with the Israeli police as lead investigator for terrorist financing and security cases, Price Waterhouse, and HSBC Israel. He lectures and publishes widely.

Acknowledgments

The editors wish to thank the Abba Eban Institute of the Interdisciplinary Center, Herzliya, Israel (IDC), for a generous grant to aid in the preparation of this book, based on a contribution to the IDC for that purpose by Mr. Michael Gross.

They wish also to thank Mr. Roy Pinchot and Dr. Barbara P. Billauer for their invaluable assistance in the final preparation of the book.

Contents

Chapter 1

Introduction

Norman A. Bailey and Bernard Touboul

The end of the Cold War confirmed the position of capitalism as the only viable and sustainable economic and societal model in a free democratic world. Globalization has accelerated, increasing the volume of trade in goods, services, capital, and information for people around the world. The expansion of the world financial bubble through financial markets' globalization and deregulation has maximized capital returns and profits. Liberal capitalism has been driven by the growing number of democratic countries, while globalization has accelerated the cyberspace transition to digital communication and artificial intelligence-based technologies.

However, globalized capitalism has generated its own problems. Capitalism offers unprecedented openness and access to markets that are both legal and illegal. For the past two decades, social, financial, and political crises have often revealed their criminal dimensions. The competitive and aggressive capitalist business model of entrepreneurs and multinational firms, the hidden interests of politicians and elites, and the endemic presence of transnational crime and terrorism are interconnected, entangled, and nowadays inseparable.

Through the complexity of the globalized flows, the capitalist world economy gives criminals the greatest means of legal and illegal enrichment ever reached on a global scale.

The convergence of interests and systematic hybridization between state and non-state actors, legal and illegal entities, criminals and terrorists as well as the integration of moral and immoral behavior has intensified.

In addition to illegal trafficking and its proceeds, criminal and terrorist organizations invest in completely legal sectors like agrobusiness, textiles, consumption goods, construction and real estate, waste treatment, entertainment, and tourism (casinos, movies, music, hotels, restaurants...). Criminal capitalism has infiltrated all aspects of our social life. The participation, assistance, and complicity of legal banks, advisors, computer scientists, lawyers, communication firms, NGOs, and charities — indeed all types of white-collar participants in complex networks — has enabled crime to penetrate and permeate the legal economy.

Through the instruments of violence, corruption, and money laundering, criminality has become a systemic driver of a globalized world in constant change. Criminality is a major source of licit and illicit financial assets' creation and one of the fundamental elements of global economics and politics, although ignored or purposely omitted from studies of these same fields.

A new economic paradigm is necessary to explain and anticipate what will be the results of this criminalization of the world economy, its actors, and instruments. Symptoms are already numerous and highly visible. The amount of dirty money infiltrated in the licit world economy is so important that it cannot be withdrawn, without causing serious damage or even collapse. Corruption affects citizens' trust in their elected representatives who are supposed to represent them and defend their interests. The social contract that must guarantee the security and equality of citizens in the face of the law loses its meaning. Legal companies poisoned by the dirty money of crime and terror alter the long-term functioning of liberal markets. Unlike the opinion of many of liberal capitalism's defenders, this infiltration is now too deep and structural for the legal system of markets to absorb and rectify.

Criminalization of the world economy has caused irreparable damage to the world and a transformation in the nature of its actors.

The entrepreneur is no longer the moral peace-seeking personage of the traditional bourgeoisie. In many cases he has become a predator acting with violence against competitors and those disturbing his plans, using illegal methods of corruption and intimidation to survive and dominate global markets.

Criminal and terrorists' activities and the dirty money they produce can no longer be ignored in the world economic models. The distinction between the legal and illegal economy is no longer relevant. Criminals invest their laundered dirty money in both legal and illegal enterprises.

Legal entrepreneurs in their turn many times behave like criminals in the name of capitalism, investing in illegal activities (tax havens, cyber piracy, collusive lobbying) to maximize profits and returns on investments. In a process of reverse money laundering, legal entities and actors even invest their licit money in illegal activities.

The convergence of interests between terrorist groups, transnational organized crime, and international mafias (from Italy, Albania/Kosovo, Turkey, China, Russia, and others) highlights the ways the terrorists use the criminals' networks and cross-border trafficking routes in order to mobilize the financing resources required for their own activities. Criminals use corruption, intimidation, and excessive violence, as do terrorists, to create, maintain, and keep their territorial criminal zones of non-governance out of reach of the law enforcement agencies and states' repressive forces.

Driven by hybridity, this new evolution of the concepts of crime and terrorism has accelerated a deep and irreversible change. Terrorists are not only using the techniques of criminals but have become essentially criminal actors while at the same time establishing legal political groups, political parties, religious groups, and companies. Like any other actors, they do not have a singular identity but a flexible, variable, and changing nature (criminal in the morning, legal businessman in the afternoon, and terrorist in the evening). This results in the complexity of untangling the interfaces between legal and illegal business activities and in the strategic cooperation between terrorist or criminal networks, legal business sectors, and governments, which has emerged in international trade and world politics.

This mutation of the world was accelerated by the end of the cold war and the resulting change in international politics' polarities. Before the end of the cold war the world was bipolar and the model of economic and political thought was binary: either capitalist or communist, either criminal or terrorist, either legal or illegal, either a moral businessman or an immoral gangster, etc. After the cold war, the world first became unipolar and then multipolar. The model of thought changed. The complexity of economic, political, and international relations intensified. Even without being a state, one can affect the interplay of international relations. One can be capitalist and socialist at the same time, or communist and liberal. One can be a terrorist with ideological preferences as well as a criminal in actions. At the same time, one can be legal and illegal.

If they do not take into account the hybridity and the variable geometry of networks of crime and terrorism, the effectiveness of policies to combat crime, corruption, money laundering, and terrorism will remain only of limited value. The criminal economy is totally globalized, while the laws combating crime and terror remain essentially territorialized. Criminal actors are categorized and labeled under unique headings: as either terrorists or criminals. Law enforcement, security, police, and judicial authorities still work from separate and different lists of suspected individuals categorized as either criminals or terrorists. They are in fact the same hybrid individuals. In other terms, one can be searched for as a criminal but may be acting as an unsearched terrorist, and vice versa. (See the case of Mohamed Merah, author in 2012 of a series of Islamist terrorist attacks committed in France in a Jewish school in Toulouse and against French soldiers in Montauban. Merah was known as a dangerous criminal but was outside the radar of the counterterrorism forces before the shootings.)

Finally, the change in the hybrid nature of crime, terror, entrepreneurial activity, and politics in a democracy results from the introduction and development of new cyber technologies. Valuable assets in our time may be intangible and immaterial. New internet trade in data and information has opened new routes of information trafficking and piracy that offer the best proceeds of criminal or terror activities. Money is generated at a level of anonymity never reached before and then injected in the world's criminal-based economy. Criminals and terrorists are like ghosts, faceless, omnipresent, anonymous, and their mass cyber-crimes affect masses of anonymous victims without any visibility or by contact with them as is the case of traditional criminal acts. Since the Enlightenment, sciences and technologies have been associated with social progress. However, today, they play a more ambiguous role in our societies. Far from being neutral, their applications and interactions with economic, political, and social factors determine their real effects. Technology is not only the creation and transformation of physical objects. It has an impact on people and society in all aspects (production, consumption, organization, communication). It changes the definition of social man and ultimately his perception of the world — and of himself. The nuclear age, environmental and climate change awareness, the ambiguous promises of molecular biology, nanotechnologies, the cyberspace of media and communication, and artificial intelligence-based computer sciences have become strong drivers of uncertainty that fuel people's fears. In this context, new sciences and technologies have brought about a profound transformation in the nature of frauds, trafficking, data and information piracy, crime with its inherent violence, and ideological or religious terrorism.

Due to global liberalization of trade and financial market's deregulation, the worldwide democratic expansion in most of the states of the world, especially in those called as such but disrespectful of the basic democratic principles, is one of the key drivers of the development of the criminal economy.

In order to exist and prosper, modern crime and terrorism are helped by the state structures of a democratic regime in several ways: first, the democratic suffrage, elections and voting systems, allow criminals and terrorists to use their social pressure on the population to offer blocs of voters to corrupt politicians in exchange for adjusted laws and favorable regulations that allow for or tolerate their illicit activities. Second, according to democratic principles, markets are open for all and any form of discrimination is rejected. Through violence, intimidation, corruption of officials in state's administration and institutions, criminals and terrorists have undue benefits from public subsidies. They can be awarded public procurement contracts and create monopolistic conditions that prevent any new entrants in their protected sectors. Third, criminals and terrorists provide jobs, healthcare, and educational services to populations in areas and territories where state governance is weak or has failed. They become appreciated and popular. Criminals and terrorists become a voting force in the democratic system, supporting chosen complaisant political candidates, or may become democratically elected officials themselves and create their own political parties as in the case of Lebanon. Fourth, banks and the financial system are a key pillar of the liberal democracies. With globalization of the illicit markets, criminals and terrorists generate an enormous amount of dirty money that needs to be laundered in order to be used in legal businesses that face limited risk from the judicial system or police. Having accomplished a legitimate existence within civil society and even favor from the elite, they can better support and develop their illicit activities. Fifth, only in liberal democracies where globalization is based on deregulation of financial and trade markets, criminals and terrorists can freely (without any patronage by the state as in Russia or China) find and buy the expert services of professional predators such as banks, financial, legal, communication, and other facilitators. These assist in laundering dirty money and also in cleansing the reputation of their criminal clients, bridging them into the legal world of economics and politics. The capitalistic business model approach of crime and terror therefore includes the 2-tiered financing methods: from "street" crimes of violent gangsters or criminals that affect the society from the bottom and from the "white-collar" crimes of competent financial, bank, business, and professional facilitators affecting the society from the top.

In addition, state repression of crime and terror in democracies has always been temporary and cyclical. In fact, criminals and terrorists often don't suffer seriously from state judicial and police repression in their established territorial zones of illegal activities. Any change in the status quo may cause a new wave of violent criminality and terrorism.

Interestingly, mafias, criminals, and terrorists have been largely eliminated from totalitarian regimes (Cosa Nostra had to escape the Italy of Mussolini, the Chinese triads fled from the China of Mao) or have been used in the patriotic and nationalistic struggle against the enemies of the state. As an opposing illustration, Emmanuel Macron, President of France, said "we shall learn how to live with terrorism". This reflects the tolerant, compromising approach of the democratic regimes, unlike that of Vladimir Putin, President of Russia, who said "Russia never negotiates with terrorists, she kills them".

Therefore, violence has become an inherent and increasingly powerful driver of the world economy and its criminalization. Organized crime and terrorism are based on violent strategies of this struggle for power through persuasion, threat, and subversion. Crime mainly uses intimidation, i.e. the fear of criminal violence directed against the citizen or organization. It is clear, for example, through the Charlie Hebdo attack in Paris, that humor, as the antidote to fear, was targeted and employees murdered. Corruption is based on greed but also on a fear of violence. However, criminal violence at this state level is discreet so as not to trigger any excessive repression that would disrupt the activities of criminal groups.

Terrorism acts violently to invalidate the state as protector and guarantor of the individuals' security. Thus, the citizen, through terrorist attacks, is doubly intimidated by violence and by the fact that its protector itself is attacked. Terrorist violence is open, visible, and its effect disseminated through mass communication. Strategically, it is the subject of prioritization, redistribution, and exceptional mobilization of the state's repressive forces. As a tactical diversion, the fight against terrorism leads to a reduction in the fight against fraudulent and criminal activities. Crime thus takes advantage of the chaos of terror to better develop its markets and better organize its fraudulent and criminal networks.

Finally, the enormous amount of dirty-laundered money engaged in all this activity has enhanced a more visible shift. The initial religious, ideological, or political grievance of terrorist groups explains its later recourse to profit-seeking criminality for financing activities and growth in influence and power. Progressively, the militant struggle gives place to a dominant motivation of easy and fast enrichment of the criminal elite assisted by their facilitators.

Through a thorough analysis and case studies on various aspects of the topic, this book will further enhance the need for a new paradigm of economic analysis, revealing and accepting the new reality of the world as a subject of systematic study.

Facilitators have become essential to the rise and spread of organized crime and terrorism. Their key function is to take advantage, through their skills and privileged positions, of all possibilities generated or tolerated by an environment created by state, legal firms, multinational enterprises, NGOs, financiers, media, the Internet, citizens as consumers, and others.

Following this introductory chapter, in Chapter 2, Bernard Touboul will highlight the role of lawyers, accountants, and auditors as well as communicators play in functioning as key operators and guardians of the rule of law. However, the engagement of reputable law firms, accounting companies, and international banks is also responsible for the establishment of off-shore and on-shore commercial structures and in operation of those structures that may facilitate illegal trafficking, corruption, and money laundering activities. Communicators use the art of communication in shaping the public opinions concerning the reputation of criminals and terrorists and, where possible, turning them into respectable citizens, legal tax-payers, and even defenders of freedom. In criminal business logic, their legal, financial, and communication advisory or consulting services are strategic instruments of crime and terror financing. They are operational facilitators operating in an environment created by other facilitators.

In Chapter 3, Yitzhak Zahavy and Yaron Hazan will explain how national icons, such as UBS, Credit Suisse, Deutsche Bank, HSBC, and many other global financial intuitions have become global laundromats for the criminal economy. They will take an up-close look at what drove financial institutions around the world to collaborate in the nefarious activities of some of their clients and by extension the use and abuse of these institutions for personal or criminal gain. They outline specific case studies to illustrate clear examples of this abuse and discuss possible remedies.

In Chapter 4, Bernard Touboul will highlight the fact that businesses are essential actors in this hybrid legal and illegal world economy. Criminal and terrorist organizations must be analyzed as enterprises and corporations pursuing their nefarious objectives through business organizational structures and strategies driven by a rational cost-benefit analysis approach in a global competitive, profit-oriented, and markets-driven world context. Usual statistical results on organized crime and terror activities may be misleading if ignoring their business logic, behavior and motivations.

In Chapter 5, Rachel Ehrenfeld will reveal that although considered the builders and pillars of Open Society, behind the militant narratives of many non-profit organizations and think-tanks are often hidden monstrous webs of criminality-enablers.

In Chapter 6, Bernard Touboul will point out that the new cyber sciences and technologies have changed the nature of social activities, including those of trafficking, crime, and terror. Today, the cyber-crime and cyber-terrorism networks are waging war through the promotion of faceless, anonymous, yet omnipresent risks, creating uncertainties in everyone's mind that enables them to influence and manipulate potential victims.

Finally, in Chapter 7, conclusion of the book, Bailey and Touboul will highlight that raising public awareness on the hybrid legal and illegal reality of the world is now a priority that should lead to a necessary paradigm shift in awareness and enforcement. The strengthened presence of the state at all levels of governance is essential to reduce the areas of opportunity increasingly left to organized crime and terrorism in their physical, political, economic, and societal conquests. These will complement the necessary repressive and deterring strategies that would be implemented by effectively naming, shaming, and destroying the reputation of all sorts of facilitators.

Chapter 2

Professional Facilitators

Bernard Touboul

The end of the Cold War marked the end of bipolarity in the balance of world powers. The world is changing with the emergence of rich and powerful non-state actors who oppose and even fight against nation states. Liberal capitalism is claiming victory as the world's only viable economic model. Corporate logic and the supremacy of markets are the drivers of today's economic, political, and social world. Protest movements and people's citizens' movements are multiplying almost everywhere to denounce the abuse of power and the sense of injustice and social inequalities in both rich and poor countries, democracies, or even totalitarian regimes (Paris and the yellow jackets, the Arab springs of the Maghreb, Hong Kong, Tehran, Beirut, and others).

Globalization has led to strategies of aggressive competition for access to resources and markets and to the frenetic increase in the speed and volume of trade in products, people, capital, and information. The goal is consumption without limits, without measure, and without borders. The financial crises of the liberal system have formalized the use of the liquidity of dirty money from crime and terrorism as a systemic and indispensable engine of the world economy and its financing.[1]

In this liberal logic with the blind aggressiveness of the markets and the obsessive search for ever greater financial returns, the satisfaction of

---

[1] Jean Cartier-Bresson, "Accounts and miscounting of the globalization of crime" ed. *The Political Economy,* 2002/2003, No. 15.

the interests of the shareholder now justifies the absence of morality in business, thus offering as many opportunities to the possessors of dirty money and their accomplices.

Mafia, organized crime, and terrorism are now structural actors in a hybrid globalization that is both legal and illegal.[2] The osmosis between globalization and their own criminal and terrorist perversion has become systemic and inescapable.[3]

The dynamics of globalization are indeed based on the capacity to create legal and illegal wealth, but also on the power to transform the illegal into legal and vice versa, by both state or non-state, institutional or individual, legitimate or informal actors. In effect, this amounts to transforming the criminal holder of dirty money into a legitimate holder in the eyes of the law. A legitimate financier may be a donor supporting terrorist causes or a saver may also be an investor investing his or her money in criminal enterprises.

There are certainly factors that facilitate crime or terrorism. For example, migratory movements and flows create community diasporas that regularly become targets, victims, but also actors and subjects of smuggling and trafficking of various products and human beings from their continents or countries of origin.[4] Another example would be the development of online video games used as money laundering platforms.[5] There are also criminal agreements, alliances, and *ententes* between mafia organizations, terrorist groups, and drug cartels that pool their networks and resources to develop their harmful projects.[6]

---

[2] Jean-Francois Gayraud, "Theorie des hybrids", CNRS Editions, 2017.

[3] Louise I. Shelley in "Dirty Entanglements: Corruption, Crime and Terrorism" (2014) concludes that corruption, crime, and terrorism will remain important security challenges in the 21 century as a result of economic and demographic inequalities in the world, the rise of ethnic and sectarian violence, climate change, the growth of technology, and the failure of nineteenth- and twentieth-century institutions to respond to these challenges when they emerged.

[4] Louise I. Shelley, "Dark Commerce: How a New Illicit Economy is Threatening Our Future", Princeton University Press (2018), p. 31.

[5] Article Business AM, 6 mars 2020, « Comment les jeux video sont le nouvel Eldorado du blanchiment d'argent ».

[6] Peng Wang, "The Crime-Terror Nexus: Transformation, Alliance, Convergence", *Asian Social Science* 6, No. 6 (2010), pp. 11–20.

However, the focus of this chapter is on actors perceived as honest, legitimate, and respectable, which have the ability to transform illegality into legality. By the same token, they create or contribute to the infiltration of the criminal into the legitimate world. The increasingly rapid movement of globalization accelerates and intensifies the hybridization between criminal/terrorist and citizen, entrepreneur, and politician.

Facilitation is an essential function for both terrorist groups and organized crime networks that must be maintained regardless of the level of their relationship (territorial cohabitation, criminal cooperation, convergence of interest, hybridization) as well as the same need for funding.

In fact, the notion of facilitators of crime and terrorism goes far beyond the mere corrupt, unscrupulous "white-collar" economic and political agents who sell their souls to the devil. It is then irrational and hypocritical to demonize only the moral perversion of a few highly publicized individuals and companies made famous by Hollywood and Netflix (Mossack & Fonseca,[7] Madoff[8]) and high-profile companies, (BCCI, Enron,[9] Wachovia Bank[10]) who are in fact guilty of having ruined rich elites who wanted to believe in the miracle of a fraudulent plan as

---

[7]Netflix movie by Steven Soderberg "The Laundromats" based on the book of Jake Bernstein *Secrecy World: Inside the Panama Papers Investigation of Illicit Money Networks and the Global Elite*, published by Henry Holt and Co. (November 21, 2017).

[8]Netflix movie by Barry Levinson "The Wizard of Lies" based on the book of the same name by Diana B. Henriques, published by St. Martin's Griffin; Reprint Edition (May 16, 2017).

[9]Issue of the *Journal of Accountancy* "The Rise and Fall of Enron — When a Company Looks Too Good to be True, It Usually Is" by C. William Thomas (April 1, 2002).

[10]Article from *The Guardian* titled "How a Big US Bank Laundered Billion USD from Mexico's Murderous Drug Gangs", April 2, 2011. The case refers to Wachovia Bank, an American bank suspected of laundering up to $378 billion of drug money from the cartels of Mexico through the fraudulent mechanism on the exchange rate of the Mexican peso. This is Wells Fargo, after acquisition of Wachovia which, after pressure by the DOJ of the USA, is sentenced to a fine of $150 million by the U.S. Justice Department. The hypothesis was widely disseminated that the consequences of sanctions to the scale of the fraud committed might cause the collapse of the bank with the risk of a new crisis in the global banking sector similar to the one that followed the bankruptcy of the financial group Lehman Brothers. The infiltration of dirty money in the economy is irreversible. Dirty money becomes untouchable.

revealed in the leaks from the Panama Papers.[11] Admittedly, the responsibility lies with these actors who facilitate criminals and terrorists in an operational way through money laundering, manipulation of figures and documents (invoices, transport contracts, awarding of public contracts), and tax, legal, and financial schemes. This is well highlighted by a Global Witness Report aired on CBS 60 minutes in January 2016 showing that ultimately, this is not about individual lawyers — it's about what is wrong with the law (both established and enforced by the same network-related lawyers) that makes it simply too easy to hide who is who and what people are doing behind anonymous shell companies.[12] There is an evolution from the elite's lawbreaking to the white-collar financial criminal.[13] But it reveals that other actors and factors assist, contribute to, and even shape the strategic and tactical environment in which these operational facilitators operate to enable the interplay of corruption, money laundering, crime, and terror.

In this context, facilitation is systemic, i.e. widespread to the point of being the key factor in the infiltration of crime and terrorism into the economy, politics, and the functioning of society.[14] Facilitation nowadays has many faces.

Some, without violence, are able to easily launder their dirty money from crime, trafficking, and political, ideological, or religious terrorism. But others help to integrate criminals and terrorists into the charitable, cultural, and political elite of society by laundering their image, reputation, and motivation in the eyes of the public and of the law.[15]

---

[11] The Panama Papers is one of the biggest leaks and largest collaborative investigations in journalism history: Files reveal the offshore holdings of 140 politicians and public officials from around the world. Current and former world leaders in the data include the prime minister of Iceland, the president of Ukraine, and the king of Saudi Arabia. More than 214,000 offshore entities appear in the leak, connected to people in more than 200 countries and territories. Major banks have assisted the creation of hard-to-trace companies in offshore havens.

[12] See https://www.globalwitness.org/shadyinc/.

[13] Arjan Reurink, "From Elite Lawbreaking to Financial Crime: The Evolution of the Concept of White-Collar Crime", Discussion Paper 16/10 of the Max Planck Institute for the Study of Societies, Cologne, September 2016.

[14] UNICRI Report "Organised Crime and the Legal Economy" (2016).

[15] Oscar Goodman, "Being Oscar: From Mob Lawyer to Mayor of Las Vegas" published by Hachette (2013) — Oscar Goodman, as America's most celebrated criminal defense attorney recounts the stories and cases of his epic life. The Mafia's go-to defender, he has

Consumers are also facilitators when they consume the products and services produced, distributed, and marketed through channels controlled by the world's mafias, organized crime, and terrorists.[16]

The media play the game of facilitating crime and terror when they arbitrarily construct the image of the terrorist, nourish and maintain the reputation of the criminal. The press gives terrorists publicity, but it often omits the propaganda message that terrorists would like to see accompanying reports of their exploits, thus reducing terrorism to mere crime or sabotage.[17]

Subjectively, they mold, manipulate, and orchestrate the collective consciousness of populations into established patterns of thought, which may approve or justify the media images of crime and terror. Nations as well as some multinational firms sponsor, finance, and use terrorists and criminals as proxies and instruments of political or commercial war to stage the conditions of their strategic and political interests.[18] The United States is one of the primary facilitators of anonymous shell companies, which are often used to fund terrorism and crime.[19] States use terrorism as a multifaceted tool, often to retain political and economic influence, and their patronage includes sanctuary, supplies, logistics, or, as is the case with Iran and Hezbollah, ideological support.[20] Multinational firms, both legal and illegal, are the actors in international and

---

tried an estimated 300 criminal cases, and won most of them. His roster of clients reads like a history of organized crime: Meyer Lansky, Nicky Scarfo, and "Lefty" Rosenthal, as well as Mike Tyson and boxing promoter Don King, along with a midget, a dentist, and a federal judge.

[16] Journalistic investigation by Nicolas Glimois titled "Dirty Money, the Poison of Finance", broadcast on French TV on January 3, 2017, https://www.youtube.com/watch?v=g3FCSRGDX8Q&t=3153s.

[17] L. John Martin, article of *The Journal of Studies in Conflict and Terrorism*, "The Media's Role in International Terrorism" (1985), pp. 127–146.

[18] Joshua Philipp, article of the *Epoch Times* titled "China Is Fueling a Drug War Against the US", January 4, 2018, reports that in an email Robert J. Bunker, Assistant Professor of research at the U.S. Army War College wrote: "The Role of China is to be a Facilitator of the Activities of Crime Between the Mexico and Latin America".

[19] Jodi Vittori, article "How Anonymous Shell Companies Finance Insurgents, Criminals, and Dictators", in *Council on Foreign Relations Journal*, dated September 7, 2017.

[20] Daniel Byman, "Deadly Connections: States That Sponsor Terrorism", Cambridge University Press (June 27, 2005).

high-frequency finance.[21] Their intra-corporate activities account for 85% of global international trade in goods and services and generate two-thirds of the world's illicit financial flows through abusive transfer pricing, misrepresentation of values, phantom corporations and transactions (the other third of illicit financial flows comes from trafficking in drugs, counterfeit goods, human beings, and in protected species of flora and fauna[22]).

Finally, the Internet and cyberspace make and keep the financing and preparation of crime and terrorism secret, hidden, and anonymous. New technologies provide an ideal environment for criminals and terrorists to develop their nefarious plans with little risk of detection or prevention by law enforcement agencies. The Internet and new technologies are preferred vehicles for propaganda (including recruitment, radicalization, and incitement to terrorism), a financing platform, simulation and training spaces, planning tools (including through covert communications and information obtained from freely accessible sources), as well as instruments of execution and cyber-attacks.[23]

Finally, the network structure of the mafia and other criminal and terrorist organizations allows for exponential growth in their activities, their effects, and the opacity through which they affect the world on a global scale.[24] Fraud and money laundering mechanisms are built on the basis of interconnected global networks of banks, real and phantom companies, and tax havens.[25]

Empirically, it seems that facilitators differ from one another according to the angle and degree of their involvement in the process of organized crime and terrorism: active and conscious militants, accomplices through complacency, influencing factors of economic, political, and societal power, victims through ignorance.

First, there are those whose vocation is itself crime, ideology, and terrorism. Those whose confirmed objective is a commitment and an

---

[21] Jean François Gayraud, « L'Art de la Guerre Financière », Ed. Odile Jacob, 2016.

[22] Raymond W. Baker, "Capitalism's Achilles Heel — Dirty Money and How to Renew the Free-Market System", Hoboken, NJ: John Wiley and Sons (2005).

[23] UNODC Report, "The Use of Internet for Terrorist Purposes" (2012).

[24] Moises Naim, "Five Wars of Globalization", *Foreign Policy*, (November 3, 2009).

[25] Damgaardt *et al.*, "Piercing the veil", Finance and Development — International Monetary Fund, June 2018. The author defines "empty shells" as legally registered companies — usually in a tax haven — but without real economic activity.

active participation in crime and terror. They are capable of defending and whitewashing criminals or terrorists and facilitating their activities because they are themselves members of the mafia family, militants of the terrorist group, administrators of the criminal enterprises. Their establishment is part of an internal strategy of the criminal, mafia, or terrorist organization. Such was the case, for example, of Oscar Goodman, a lawyer for the mob and mayor of Las Vegas who was devoted to the families of New York's Cosa Nostra. This is also the case of law firms that defend banks or institutions in countries subject to sanctions or embargoes.[26] Their role is to keep illicit activities behind a smokescreen or within a legal and financial framework that effectively complies with a law favorable to crime. They know how to act while remaining out of the reach of law enforcement surveillance and repression. Their skills guarantee the resources necessary for the complex set-up of off-shore and on-shore companies, the accounting manipulation of money laundering, the penetration of circles and art markets open to illicit financial flows, and their advocacy and defense skills in the face of justice. Their studies are financed by dirty or criminal money and they are graduates of the best and most prestigious universities in the world. They enjoy a network of political and financial influence beyond suspicion, infiltrate the jet set, and finally influence and are part of a social elite with uniform and molded values that no one, by definition, questions.[27]

There are also the hidden beneficiaries of crime and terrorism. In the shadows they can both facilitate their existence and increase their repression. They sponsor activities and orchestrate the harmful effects to satisfy their interests, sometimes in the very name of "raison d'état". They are the states, governments, political parties, and elites and multinational corporations that instrumentalize, sponsor, and commit criminal and terrorist acts to advance their geopolitical interests, to influence public opinion, and to shape their vision of the world.[28] For example,

---

[26] Article of *The Economist*, June 20, 2015, "Who are you calling a Rogue" — one case among many today, Sarosh Zaiwalla is an arbitrator in court in London who defended the Mellat Bank of Iran blacklisted by Britain for alleged participation to the nuclear programme of Iran.

[27] Jean-François Gayraud, « Le Monde des Mafias: Géopolitique du crime organisé », Ed. Odile Jacob, 2005.

[28] By way of illustration, we can cite the history of the 5th Republic in France and the use of extremist and criminal militants of the Service d'Action Civique (SAC) created by the

national states sponsor terrorist organizations: Iran created and still maintains Hezbollah.[29] Pro-Iranian Lebanon supports the financing of the Hezbollah terrorist group through the laundering of drug trafficking money.[30] Russia was using the effects of the Russian mafia to weaken Ukraine before a military aggression in 2014.[31] China supports Latin American drug cartels to oppose the capitalist economic development model imposed on the southern states by the West.[32] In the 1980s, a wave of attacks on banks in France and Belgium made it possible to finance political parties in Europe and to arm revolutionary and terrorist groups (Baader Gang or Rote Armee Fraktion, Red Brigades,[33] ETA…). Their actions terrorized public opinion, which in the end could only choose the reassuring security and social order of democratic liberalism and the

---

General De Gaulle to repress political opposition, particularly communist, but also used as an intermediary between the political elite, the state police, and banditry, whose income was used to finance the political parties in power until the mid-1980s.

[29] Ben Hubbard, article of the *New York Times*, "Iran Out to Remake Mideast With Arab Enforcer: Hezbollah", August 27, 2017.

[30] Emanuele Ottolenghi, "Lebanon Is Protecting Hezbollah's Cocaine Trade in Latin America", June 15, 2018, from Foundation for Defense of Democracies and published in *Foreign Policy* magazine.

[31] Ralph D. Thiele, "Hybrid Threats and how to counter them", published in *ISPSW*, March 2016, No. 448. The author explains the example of the Russian action in Crimea and in Ukraine in 2014 highlighting the Russian hybrid threats and their non-military instruments. They demonstrate an impressive performance in parallel to the use of the military instruments. This includes investments and the targeted Russian trade of goods and services, as well as the capital used to influence the major economic and political elites. The media participated in support of political parties hostile to European integration, and therefore pro-Russian. Links between the elements of the local crime of Ukraine and of Crimea and the organized crime of Russia have been noticed, as well as links between religious institutions. Current ethnic tensions with campaigns for "the right of minorities" have been exploited to exacerbate economic and social inequalities. Finally, selected targets have been hit by massive and coordinated cyber-attacks.

[32] The *Epoch Times* article titled "The terrorists might use the drug cartels to enter the United States", February 3, 2016, which cites that according to a report from November 2015 at the US–China Economic Security Review Commission, the Chinese regime has in Latin American governments that economic development can be achieved without bending to Western bans and without sharing the "American objectives of regional stability and good governance".

[33] Jean-François Gayraud, « Le Monde des mafias: Géopolitique du crime organisé », Ed. Odile Jacob, 2005, pp. 139, 362–363.

political parties that defend it. The use of criminal violence and terrorist techniques still allows, even in our Western democracies, the silencing of political contests or the claims of identity and religion, still a credo of the independence and libertarian struggles. Or again, industries and multinational firms, including those in the luxury goods, textile, agri-food, and electronics sectors, buy more or less directly products and services resulting from organized crime and terrorism (diamond financing conflicts, unhealthy conditions in rare metal mines,[34] animal fur trafficking, forced exploitation of the labor of women, children,[35] immigrants, and others).

And, there are the professionals and experts who know, master, and navigate the weaknesses and vulnerabilities in the laws, governance systems, and technical and administrative procedures of the institutions and their operations. They enable criminals and terrorists to take advantage of them, as if they were ordinary clients. They do not kill, they do not steal, but they help them for a variety of motives: gambling, money, vices, social position, profits from unfair competition obtained through intimidation, and corruption of competitors, complacency, negligence, and cowardice, or simply opportunism when immoralism, especially political immoralism, becomes the norm. They are consulting and law firms, accountants and financiers, business management experts specializing in the complex set-up of shell companies and tax optimization,[36] banks

---

[34]Article of Charles Lavery in Sunday Mail, "Plight of African child slaves forced into mines — for our mobile phones", July 6, 2008 — The child miners of the Democratic Republic of Congo (DRC) risk death to dig for a highly dangerous ore used in mobiles, laptops and games consoles. Coltan smuggling is big business throughout Africa and is a major source of income for warring militias. Coltan, which is highly toxic, is also blamed for birth defects in the areas where it is mined. The UN Security Council has cited 85 international companies for their purchases of natural resources from warring factions in the country, though the firms claim they are "unaware" where their coltan is mined. The UN list includes household names such as Compaq, Dell, IBM, Nokia, and Siemens.

[35]Article in *The Guardian*, November 24, 2016, "Child labour is part of most of what we buy today: what can we do"?

[36]Ben Hallman, *et al.*, article of the ICIJ (International Consortium of Investigative Journalists), "Western Advisers Helped an Autocrat's Daughter Amass and Shield A Fortune", January 19, 2020, explain how regulators around the globe have virtually ignored the key role Western professionals, particularly the Big Four PwC, Boston Consulting Group, Ernst and Young, Deloitte, play in maintaining an off-shore industry

of all types whether central, depository, investment, intermediary, or other banks,[37–39] businessmen experienced in international trade techniques, professionals in financial systems and high-frequency finance.[40] All of these are legitimate, but they are all sufficiently skilled to know how to surf the boundaries between legal and illegal.

Finally, there are consumers of both products and information who, through ignorance, influence, or manipulation, develop blind and irresponsible consumer behavior. How did they accidentally become financiers of crime and terrorism?[41] By buying a counterfeit product, by wearing a jewel whose gold is extracted by children in slavery, by buying the stock of a publicly traded company whose objectives serve the interests of the mafia. They thus participate in the design of organized crime and terrorism while defending, albeit sincerely, humanist and moral values. They absorb the information available through the Internet and its global service providers and through the agency of the press and media. Their personal belief system is thus shaped into a collective consciousness that helps to redefine good and evil. They buy products whose manufacturing, distribution and marketing chains are under the control of mafia and terrorist groups,[42] whether they are aware of it or are negligent. They claim the values of fair trade without knowing the real conditions of production of global industries such as textiles, food processing, or electronics.

---

that drives money laundering and drains trillions from public coffers. https://www.icij.org/investigations/luanda-leaks/western-advisers-helped-an-autocrats-daughter-amass-and-shield-a-fortune/.

[37] *Los Angeles Times* (Associated Press), "Chinese Banks a Haven for Web Counterfeits", May 11, 2015, https://www.bangkokpost.com/business/555623/chinese-banks-a-haven-for-web-counterfeits.

[38] Bloomberg, January 16, 2015, "One Thing Gangs Smuggling Latin Migrants Over the Border Can't Do Without: Big U.S. Banks", https://www.bloomberg.com/news/articles/2015-01-16/one-thing-gangssmuggling-latin-migrants-over-the-border-can-t-do-without-big-u-sbanks.

[39] The Jamestown Foundation, a global research and analysis think-tank, already in 1995 published in Volume 1, Issue 101, that 40% of the Russian economy is controlled by the Russian mafia, two-thirds of banks are under mafia control.

[40] Jean François Gayraud, « L'Art de la Guerre Financière », Ed. Odile Jacob, 2016.

[41] Article of David Povey, "Are You Accidentally Funding Terrorism?" in the *Journal of the International Compliance Association*, July 1, 2019.

[42] Hannah Roberts, article of the *Financial Times*, "How the Mafia Got to Our Food", November 8, 2018.

So, whom do we ultimately accuse of being a facilitator? Because this responsibility has great ramifications. Many people and governments of the world are now subject to the phenomena of organized crime and terrorism, to their will and to their harmful effects. Many are at the point where their governments admit that they are incapable of remedying the situation and have capitulated in the face of the complexity of the problem,[43] a corruption that is too deeply rooted in society and its institutions, the political immoralism common to all kinds of regimes and powers, and the cost/benefit business logic common to both legitimate and illegitimate actors. Despite all the institutional, financial, and human efforts made at international level, the fight and repression against organized crime and terrorism have had only a limited impact. The conclusion is obvious. The estimation of the results of this struggle is disturbing and disappointing: less than 1% of the global illicit financial flows is currently seized and frozen according to the FATF's report of 2011. Europol confirmed in 2017, in its latest report on trends and developments in the fight against financial crime, that the record of the global fight against money laundering is disappointing. The level of seizures of money laundered still does not exceed 1%, and that, notwithstanding both the repressive and preventive measures of the international conventions, agreements, and cooperation mechanisms.

The importance of crime and terrorism facilitation, as long as it is associated with and perceived only from the perspective of white-collar criminals, is still ignored or minimized because it does not resort to the violence which is characteristic of organized crime or terrorism.

For a long time, law and justice only addressed the operational actors of crime and terrorism, the workers or "blue-collar" criminals, those who get their hands dirty. White collar criminals and terrorists, on the contrary, are people with respectable jobs. They do not kill, they do not steal, they act through the use of documents and information, and are close to the decision-makers, elites, political leaders, and the most powerful business people.

For a long time, law enforcement has not targeted these so-called "white-collar" operational facilitators because their crimes are not violent in nature and usually involve some form of deception, forgery, or fraud for financial gain. These crimes include credit card fraud, insurance and

---

[43] Josefina Salomón, article of *InSight Crime Journal*, "Argentina Customs 'Mafia' Earns Millions from China Imports", November 27, 2019.

personal data fraud, identity theft, money laundering, immigration fraud, tax evasion,[44] high-frequency finance, financial vehicles and market securitization, and others[45] – methods that require discretion, secrecy, and invisibility so that criminals and terrorists can continue to act, prepare their activities, or maintain their political and ideological movement without being disturbed, detected, or prevented by law enforcement agencies.

However, criminals and terrorists still have to be distinguished. Mafia and organized crime, by a business and profit logic, need investment and funding to stay in the shadows. They do not confront the state, avoid being the centre of attention of law enforcement agencies, and do not seek media exposure.

Terrorism, on the contrary, is a crime of a different complexity. It requires planning, human resources to execute, an effective communications and media network, and an executive to manage and oversee any activity in order to achieve the desired impact. This means a considerable amount of funds are needed to develop their macabre plan, to recruit and train human resources, to acquire logistics, weapons, and trafficked items to be exchanged. They also need to coordinate and communicate globally, ensure field activity, and establish a command centre. This requires the acquisition of equipment and real estate, important sources of intelligence and information to thwart anti-terrorist organizations, and therefore the channeling of the necessary finances through ways and techniques that must go unnoticed.

The use of white-collar facilitators is therefore ideal since it allows for theft, laundering, and the appropriation of money in a non-violent and secret manner. The enormous amount of funds needed is met through the multiple resources in which these operational white-collar facilitators play an important role, even if money from violent criminality, various trafficking, and street crimes including kidnapping for ransom, extortion, and others is added. Financial and non-violent crime accounts for two-thirds of illicit financial flows worldwide. One-third corresponds to income from violent forms of crime.[46]

---

[44] Sadia Basharat, article in *Eurasia Review Magazine*, "Exploring the Link Between White Collar Crime and Terrorism — Op-ed", May 2, 2018.

[45] Jean-François Gayraud, "Le nouveau capitalisme criminel », Ed. Odile Jacob, 2014.

[46] Raymond W. Baker, "Capitalism's Achilles Heel — Dirty Money and How to Renew the Free-Market System", Hoboken, NJ: John Wiley and Sons (2005). In 2005, Baker estimates that $500 million was derived from abusive transfer pricing in intra-company

These white-collar facilitators, transforming illegality into legality and vice versa, are lawyers, accountants, professional hackers for the security of legal corporate systems. They are also bankers, financiers, business advisors, legitimate business leaders, politicians, or local elected officials. They use public relations and branding agencies. They act under the guise of NGOs whose regulations for their establishment and operations are often lax, negligent, and not very diligent. They own or manage casinos, gambling and betting companies, real estate and land, and are art and antique dealers. Many are people of high respectability and social status who commit criminal offenses in the course of their trade and professional practice.

Facilitators are legitimate and operational. They apply the law to the best of their ability, particularly in off-shore and on-shore tax haven states whose banking, financial, and business laws are designed to be lax and favorable to financial crime. They make it easy, hidden, and even secret to use legal means, in accordance with flexible laws, to develop, for example, a shell company that would secretly work as the financial department of a criminal or terrorist enterprise. They sell their technical skills, legal know-how, access to their networks of influence, or even the established and legal framework of their business to criminals and terrorists to the detriment of law and morality. They inject laundered money into legitimate economic channels through appropriate legal and fiscal arrangements. They plead, build, and demonstrate the charitable or laudable reputation of criminals and terrorists, even though their clients may have been charged. They know how to channel legitimate funds into humanitarian, educational, or social structures and projects that terrorists sponsor, manage, and manipulate as sources of funding and propaganda through the media and social networks around the world.

They are the technicians who make it possible for organized crime and transnational terrorism to infiltrate the economy. This infiltration is based on threats of violence, on the corruption of officials and employees, but above all on the use of financial resources that these facilitators manipulate. They carry out international control operations and buy out companies with financing of illicit origin. They pay and transfer funds to companies supporting crime and terrorism. They organize charitable

---

transactions, $250 million from phantom transactions, and $250 million from false declarations of commercial value of the total estimated $1600 million in illicit financial flows in 2001.

donations through formal and informal banking channels. They design and participate in the financing of criminal trade activities (money laundering through international trade operations). Finally, with the complacency of many banks, they infiltrate the international financial markets with dirty money through high-frequency finance, financial vehicles, and market securitization.[47]

The state, the multinational corporations (banking, financial, manufacturing, or services), legal, Information Technology, financial, tax service providers, as well as complacent or careless SMEs, NGOs naïve or negligent about the origin of donors and their money, and the consumers, as key players in liberal capitalism, are as much facilitators as they are accomplices and stakeholders in organized crime and terrorism, while remaining legitimate and compliant with the law.

This phenomenon of hybridization of globalization[48] (legal and illegal at the same time depending on the context and the need) to which the globalization of markets and the crises it has led us to today leads to a generalized consent and trivialization of the negative effects of crime and terrorism, and even a certain recognition of its political and socio-economic impact often in substitution for bankrupt local, regional, and international governance.

Consequently, instead of demonizing the facilitators and other accomplices of crime and terror, these actions should be seen as a mutation in the world where state and non-state actors today share governance.

Mafia groups, organized crime, and terrorists have become influential actors in national decision-making processes and influence public authorities at different levels of governance, thanks to their infiltration of business, institutional, and political circles. Previously, the non-state actor was ineligible to take part in power decisions because they were marginal and reprehensible. Today, these same actors offer a complementarity to the state, they are legitimized with a public utility function (crime money is injected into the rescue of the world economy, fear of terror incites voters to choose the peaceful comfort of liberal democracy). They offer subsidiarity to the state in countries where the governing public authority is vulnerable or bankrupt.

---

[47]Yepes, Verdugo, "International Cooperation in the Fight against Terrorist Financing", Dissertation, 2008, Universita de Barcelona, p. 56.

[48]Jean-François Gayraud, "Théorie des hybrides", CNRS Editions, 2017.

In support of the idea of a new economic paradigm,[49] the struggle between state and non-state and hybrid actors (both legitimate and illegitimate) seems outdated. A new approach to the economy is emerging: criminals and terrorists in their logic of business, markets, and power contribute to and even impose themselves in the mediation between democracy and capitalism. States now include money from crime and trafficking in the calculation of their GDP (11% of GDP in France, 19% on average in Europe,[50] 50% in Albania[51]).

The state has recognized the authority of crime and terrorism to the point of declaring war on them, of having recourse to them on certain occasions, of using laundered money to remedy financial crises. States, public authorities, and populations have given their consent to this new criminal and terrorist governing authority since they consume the products and services of the crime and terror industry within the prescribed rules of liberal capitalism.

The facilitation of crime and terrorism through white-collar facilitators and other legitimate accomplices and stakeholders is a symptom of a changing world, of a hybridization of globalization when legality and illegality interact with each other in a permanent osmosis. Crime and terror have evolved from being marginal factors in society, to actors of influence, and now even to the authoritative stage of local, regional, and international governance.

As an illustration in West Africa and the Sahel, the abandonment of the state in its governance role leaves a vacuum that crime and terror are only waiting to fill. Lawless zones are multiplying in the vast areas of desert and forests where criminal gangs and highwaymen can freely hide, move about or escape. They impose their law by force, terror, and weapons on the areas they seek to control.[52]

They assert their authority over sequestered populations, forced to submit to the laws of a religion or morality that the actors do not necessarily even apply to themselves.

---

[49] N. Bailey and B. Touboul, "Is Criminality the New Economic Paradigm?", *The International Economy*, Spring, 2019.

[50] Article RTL, Marie Pierre Hadda, https://www.rtl.fr/actu/conso/prostitution-et-argent-sale-pourquoi-l-italie-et-le-royaume-uni-les-integrent-au-calcul-de-leur-pib-7772357833.

[51] Jean-François Gayraud, « Le Monde des Mafias: Géopolitique du crime organisé », Odile Jacob, 2005, pp. 88–89.

[52] FIDH, Investigation Report, « Dans le centre du Mali, les populations prises au piège du terrorisme et du contreterrorisme », November 2018/727F.

They run the criminal business of gangs and private armies as professional mercenaries and looters under the pretext of tribal or ethnic rivalries with common practices of kidnapping for ransom, torture, and extortion.[53] They spread fear and terror through special operations, military guerrillas, raids behind the identity flag of a religion (and the one that is scary today is Islam!). They exist and act thanks to the financing of sponsoring states such as Saudi Arabia, Qatar, Iran who see the opportunity to convey an ideology through the fear they develop. They act under the influence and funding of local governments, which thus put pressure on the political opposition.

They provoke the expropriation and forced displacement of populations in order to gain access to resources, goods, and even slaves.[54] The governmental social contract does not exist anymore in these areas. Recourse to state justice no longer makes sense and leaves room for spontaneous popular reprisals and arbitrary justice. In these lawless zones, the trafficking and smuggling of goods, people, and money in transit to the consumer markets of Europe and the world is under the control of terrorists, bandit *jihadists*, and organized criminals.[55] Then our technical facilitators take over the task of channeling the proceeds of crime to known money laundering places from the Maghreb to Europe and from the United States to China. This infernal machine feeds itself through the nexus of facilitators that cements the gangster-state to corruption, organized crime/terror, and to the business, financial, and political communities and circles.

The socio-economic and political governance of the state is relayed to these other forms of non-state authority such as multinationals, NGOs, and civil society but also mafias, organized criminals, and terrorists who have the control, the power of influence, and the ability to take part in geopolitical decision-making in most cases for similar objectives of profit, power, and participation in the project of liberal capitalism.

---

[53] Aïssatou Diallo, Article on « Trafic d'armes, orpaillage, braconnage… Cartographie du financement des groupes armés », in *Jeune Afrique Magazine*, December 19, 2019.

[54] In West Africa, the societal structure is based on a system of ethnic groups which are themselves sub-divided into castes, including "slaves by heredity or descent" — for an illustration, see https://observers.france24.com/fr/20190923-mali-esclavage-homme-malmene-ligote-public.

[55] Tawfik Hamel, article on « Djihadisme: Sahel, où se rencontrent terrorisme et criminalité », April 2017, in *The Maghreb and Orient Courier*, https://lecourrierdumaghrebetdelorient.info/jihadism/djihadisme-le-sahel-ou-se-rencontrent-terrorisme-et-criminalite.

© 2021 World Scientific Publishing Company
https://doi.org/10.1142/9789811229138_0003

Chapter 3

Financial Facilitators

Yitzhak Zahavy and Yaron Hazan

Banks and financial services have always been the preferred platform for laundering illicit funds; the ability to manage large volumes of money, transfer it from one bank to another and from one country to another fits well with criminals' and terrorists' goals. Criminals and terrorists seek faster ways to collect and share value, transfer it between countries in a safe way, safe from the eyes of the regulators, police, and security organizations.

Sanctions are an economic tool for punishing an entity that is involved in non-legitimate activity. Sanctions may forbid business activity with countries, organizations, and/or individuals; limit them to specific types of activity, such as humanitarian, or even allow the activity under certain reporting conditions, such as the "Conflict Minerals Act" rule that allows companies to buy specific minerals from conflict zones as long as they report and declare they do so. A specific dilemma in the early 2000s was related to the US Office of Foreign Assets Control ("OFAC") sanctions against Iran. Banks in the US were not allowed to maintain business relationships with Iranian banks.

Do these requirements apply in other jurisdictions? Should a bank in the UK limit its activity to avoid relationships with Iranian banks if the UK law allows it? The large banks with a global footprint had to decide if they are going to adopt a global or country-specific policy. Such an approach is practical as many countries publish lists of restricted entities.

The problem was compounded when the Iranian banks tried to transfer US dollars through their accounts in Europe. In such cases, the funds must be cleared through the US as part of the inter-bank clearing process. Such a request could cause the European banks to violate the US sanctions, so the two sides decided to avoid the problem by not including the fact that the transactions originated in Iranian banks.

In order to avoid the detection of Iranian entities in the screening tools applied in their US operations, the European banks also asked the Iranian banks not to include in the free text fields the names of the customers. All of this activity was engaged in for the purpose of hiding the information from the US Authorities, structuring the messages to include minimum information, and bypassing the sanctions-related controls.

Reading this story today sounds like a criminal activity conducted by the banks, but we tend to judge past cases with current norms; today, none of this could have happened, while in 2001 it was a common practice.

Such behavior reflects the approach that global banks implemented and their view of financial crime risk management as a derivative of the activity.

The evolvement of regulation and enforcement, together with the progress in compliance practice and understanding of the regulatory expectation, makes it almost impossible for banks today to decide not to comply with the sanction's regime. The lessons were learned and global banks apply such global policies with strict controls to ensure sanctions violations are not part of their day-to-day business activity.

In the third decade of the 21st century, banks do not deliberately violate the law; they try to be effective in their compliance controls and follow the specific requirements. Is this good enough? Does this mean that money laundering has been effectively confronted?

Unfortunately, not. Globalization made the ability to move funds and goods faster, easier and safer; the growth, volume of data, and the pace of transactions means everything is on a larger scale, including crime and terror. In short, the globalized economy enables global financial crime. Customers expect all services to be provided through digital channels; many Fin-tech initiatives help banks keep up with the digitalization, but compliance-related controls have never been a priority.

The reality is that criminals and terrorists know exactly what banks are doing, which banks are stricter, and how to most effectively enter the financial system.

Criminals and terrorists may differ in their motivation and resources, but learn from each other how to manage their financial resources. They recruit lawyers, accountants, data experts, real-estate professionals, and others to identify weaknesses in the financial sector.

Why are the banks losing this battle? Why do important international banks, such as Deutsche Bank, Wells-Fargo, Den Danske Bank, and Bank Hapoalim in Israel continue to be heavily fined for continuing to launder money? AML/TF Transaction Monitoring systems are one explanation:

Banks use rules-based scenarios to monitor their customers' activity, these rules are binary — if a certain transaction exceeds a certain amount, an alert is generated. As in the case of the Sanctions regime, where all names are published and the perpetrators know if they should avoid using a specific name, the rules are well known to them, so they know what type of transaction to avoid.

Any compliance expert who used such systems will testify these are a waste of time and budget, and research shows up to 99% false positives as an industry ratio; it will never work because it is not designed to serve the purpose, for the following reasons:

1. Money laundering is a crime that is related to financing another crime — if you believe rules can detect these crimes, you should create specific rules for human trafficking/drug dealing/terrorism, etc. Each of these crimes includes several kinds of operations, including types of financial activity — so you will need several rules for each predicate offense — all the rule-based systems are in fact designed to ignore most of the activities and alert only specific thresholds. Are these rules and thresholds related to the predicate offenses? In a word, No.
2. The FATF standards acknowledge that banks are the private sector gate-keepers and as such can only control the data they own and collect; therefore, the expectation is that the banks will properly conduct the Know Your Customer ("KYC") process and detect unusual activity. Are these rules-based systems tuned to detect the customers' unusual behavior? The answer again is No.

Rules-based detection is ineffective; sophisticated criminals know how it works and demonstrate legitimate activity. The distinction is no longer binary. Enforcement cannot be effective using a binary approach.

Rules that separate legitimate behavior from suspicious behavior belong to the past, relying as they do on a narrow perspective of reality.

Criminals and terrorists understand the weaknesses of the banks' controls and easily find the ways to bypass them. A good recent example was given the name of the "Russian Laundromat" and demonstrates how easy it was for money launderers to transfer billions of Euros/Dollars without detection or reporting to the regulators.

The people behind the scheme opened shell companies in European countries, registered them as legitimate "low risk" entities per AML controls, as they know which industries would trigger "high risk" and Enhanced Due Diligence ("EDD"). The companies were registered in accordance with relevant law, names of managers and directors were provided, in such a way that no screening system could possibly alert that something was wrong.

Most of these companies were shell companies, meaning that no real business activity was ever performed by them.

Once business relationships with the European banks were established, these sophisticated money launderers started moving funds from Russia, Latvia, and a few other countries to the UK and other Western European countries. They knew how the transaction monitoring tools are designed and they increased their activity slowly over time; they reached a target number of a few hundred six-digit amounts; around half a million British pounds being transferred from originating accounts to a destination account each month.

The next phase was to transfer the money using foreign currency exchange services; meaning sending USD from Latvia to the UK for example. The clearing process showed the receiving bank's monitoring systems clearing all funds arriving from US, a low risk country, and the bank involved was always an American bank, which used the clearing process.

As simple as it sounds, it meant that the controls in place missed one of the most important risk indicators: the source of funds.

Needless to say, none of these "customers" reported the real originating countries as their countries of operations, none of them used Hedging services to defend against losses embedded in currency exchange rates, all of these seemingly non-rational behaviors serving only one purpose — to keep up the flow of millions of pounds each month without being asked too many questions.

Is this still possible?

Yes. While banks are investing more in their KYC process, they rely mainly on the information provided by the customer. For sophisticated money launderers, creating shell companies and registering them in the "Company House" or other registries will ensure that new type of controls will show the bankers the innocent picture they wish to present.

The challenge for the criminals remains the same: they need to find a specific bank that will be easy to enter, and once they are in, it is a question of structuring the activity to remain below the radar in order to get to the "layering" phase of the money laundering process.

In a globalized economy, the main platform for banks to stay the reliable and relevant channel for cross-border payments is correspondent banking. This network of banks can survive only if banks can rely on each other's controls and trust each other to manage their own risks.

The missing capability that would enable banks to effectively trace their correspondent banking activity should be based on machine learning that can analyze many details at the same time and detect changes in behavior in a certain path, coming from a certain source or using a certain bank as intermediary.

Banks have recently invested significant resources in improving their compliance programs. They recruited experienced people from various relevant disciplines, and keep improving their controls' effectiveness. Global banks have implemented global standards when realizing that searching after the weak links on a country or regional basis is not effective, since the battlefield is not limited to any jurisdiction.

Regulators are beginning to understand that current methods have failed and, in some countries, they are also collaborating with the banks to raise the bar and set new standards for compliance effectiveness.

A View to the Future

Banks and regulators are usually one step behind the criminals. While they are starting to understand what to do, the methods of laundering money or funding terrorism are constantly changing.

Criminals understand banks will not keep on using their ineffective controls, especially when new technologies enable them to find anomalies in the data and detect unusual behavior. Criminals can bypass certain controls, but they cannot always make criminal activity look completely normal.

The next stage in this ongoing game is a mixture of several old and new phenomena:

– *Multiplayer video games*
  The ability to communicate verbally without being exposed to wire-tapping was an area terrorists and criminals identified as a safe zone, the ability to open an account using traditional payments methods and then let other "players" pay you for drugs through this platform is easy.

– *Fantasy sports*
  Fantasy leagues are legal and not considered as "gambling" according to exemption of US gambling laws that label DFS (Daily Fantasy Sport) competitions as "games of skill" rather than chance, all that a terrorist group or organized crime syndicate needs to do is to arrange a group of people, open a DFS competition, and start moving funds: how much, at what price, who checks if such a group rewarded a member by winning, etc. They may decide each week who won based on his success in drug dealing!

– *Luxury cars*
  In many countries there are no reporting obligations for car dealers. Criminals pay large sums in cash and buy their Lamborghini. This market serves the Integration phase of money laundering, but it can also be a phase in the process for criminals, not only to hide the source of funds, but to make more profits as well.

  If someone buys a Ferrari in Vancouver, he can transfer the funds from any tax haven or weak-regime bank account, and even claim the VAT back. The banks in Canada will not see the source of funds as they arrive in US dollars through the clearing system.

– *Fine art and antiquities*
  This is a non-regulated area. Dealers do not have any reporting obligation; large amounts of money can be transferred between individuals without any relation to the actual value of the object. Dealers can sell a piece of art for a million dollars even if the actual worth is a hundred dollars, the buyer actually paying for something else (weapons/drugs/human trafficking). Why is this so easy? Confidentiality, portability, and price volatility. These three characteristics explain why art is one of the preferred money laundering vehicles.

– *Crowdfunding*
Crowdfunding is a platform to donate or lend money for a specific purpose. Who can prove the purpose stated is the real purpose? Maybe it is ISIS collecting donations. Maybe it serves a drug cartel. The volumes and values are getting bigger every year. Some of it is legitimate, serving noble causes, which is exactly the company preferred by money launderers and terrorism financiers.

– *Capital market trading*
Moving large sums using the capital markets products is easy. Two partners can decide to sell each other over the counter the securities they hold, set a price for ensuring they will get it or even trade with each other and layer the funds.
How many websites offer platforms for securities trading options or foreign exchange? Do they have enough knowledge of their customers' source of funds? Or maybe they are owned indirectly by criminals? Banks have more experience in this and still struggle to do it right; those entities that are less experienced in risk-management practices can serve criminals as "the door" to the legitimate financial system.

– *Trade-Based Money Laundering (TBML)*
This old method is making a BIG comeback. TBML has always been preferred by criminals. Terrorist groups have used this method from the days of the IRA (hiding weapons in furniture/hiding cash in goods). Supervision is expected to be enforced through several channels — Public (customs/border controls) and Private (Shipping companies, vessels, and banks).
Someone has created a unique machine that can predict cancer, what is the value? Can he ship the prototype to "investors", and they will pay him $200 million? Whose responsibility will it be to stop this transaction? The banks? Customs? The shipping companies? It is a fact that very few commercial, financial, and criminal frauds and trafficking are detected by customs all over the world.

– *Cryptocurrencies/blockchain*
This is the best way to transfer value and stay anonymous — buying drugs or paying for human trafficking on the dark web. We believe that the older crypto-currencies (such as Bitcoin) will disappear or lose most of their value. New currencies that are created to be aligned with AML requirements will survive, and maintain their usefulness to the criminal and terrorist organizations.

In conclusion, the financial industry as a "gate keeper" has failed. The private banking sector could not protect humanity from the financial activity of criminal syndicates. The mixture between legal and illegal activities is a fact; many terrorists and criminals have found their path into legitimate business activities, thus making it even harder to detect their activity.

Banks started working with regulators to enhance their controls. Compliance is more professional and new technologies enable the financial sector to fight back. Still, the banking system continues to be vulnerable because of weak or suborned banks. Sophisticated criminals that understand the weaknesses and the gaps in the system can still find their way into it.

The new methods create new problems, but they still use the banking system, either at the placement, layering, or the integration phases.

In the next few years, criminals and terrorists will increase the use of these new channels. Banks will struggle to fight back, will rely on AML controls conducted by their counterparties and the complexity of the risks will make it almost impossible to effectively manage them.

Two main trends can make the difference:

1. As soon as regulators from different countries, different banks, and different law enforcement agencies will effectively cooperate, then criminals and terrorists will face a real challenge.
2. The more banks and regulators adopt new technologies that support a holistic view of reality and risks, the more effective their compliance programs will be. Until now, the authorities have been playing poker with criminals who can see their cards. Digitalization or digital transformation is already part of the banks' vision to increase business activity. Regulation technology should be adapted in parallel to increase the safety of the system.

Appendix: Effective Detection of Risks

What then is the way to do better? To invest in effective methods, our criteria for determining effective methods would be, for example:

1. **Completeness**: In order to detect unusual behavior, banks need to use a multi-dimensional view of the activity, look at all customers at any time.

2. **Anomalies provide a holistic view of risks**: look at all the customers' characteristics and activities.
3. **A multi-dimensional view is meaningful**: when you get a rules-based alert start asking questions and decide if the answers are credible. Regardless of the rule or scenario triggering the alert, in a multi-dimensional view you must start with clarity about the combination of behavior characteristics.
4. **Contextualized detection**: view the changes in behavior compared to the customer himself and the population at the same time.

Case Study: HSBC Bank

In December 2012, the US Department of Treasury along with the Financial Crimes Enforcement Network (FinCen), the Office of the Comptroller of the Currency (OCC), and the Office of Foreign Assets Control (OFAC) announced that they achieved a collective agreement with HSBC Bank Plc and its affiliates (HSBC) in which the bank management admitted they violated several criminal laws.[1]

HSBC agreed to pay a $1.9 billion fine and agreed to sign a DPA — Deferred Prosecution Agreement.

A Monitor was appointed for a period of five years to closely review HSBC's progress and implementation of appropriate controls to fight money laundering, terrorist financing, and sanctions violations.

The detailed agreement was the first of its kind and revealed some severe misconduct by HSBC employees and management, admitting to:

1. Cooperation with sanctioned countries, sanctioned business entities, and sanctioned individuals — by designing their Financial transactions to avoid sanctions-related controls, enabling smooth transfer of funds, and ignoring the OFAC sanctions regime.

    The settlement included violations of the following:

    (a) The Iranian Transactions Regulations (ITR), 31 C.F.R. part 560.
    (b) The Burmese Sanctions Regulations (BSR), 31 C.F.R. part 537.
    (c) The Sudanese Sanctions Regulations (SSR), 31 C.F.R. part 538.
    (d) The Cuban Assets Control Regulations (CACR), 31 C.F.R. part 515.
    (e) The Libyan Sanctions Regulations (LSR), 31 C.F.R. part 550 (which were in force until 2004).

---

[1] https://www.treasury.gov/press-center/press-releases/Pages/tg1799.aspx.

2. Cooperation with drug cartels by ignoring the ownership of accounts in Mexico, ignoring the volume and value of funds deposited, defining the financial activity as "low risk", and in case of any transaction monitoring alerts by the monitoring systems, ignoring these alerts and adding them to a pile of "back-log" documents.

    (a) HSBC rated Mexico as having "standard" money laundering risk, the lowest of the bank's four possible country risk ratings. This rating was given contrary to the evidence suggesting a higher risk rating. As a result of ratings like this, hundreds of billions of dollars in wire transactions from Mexico were excluded from the bank's internal AML reviews. The bank also did not monitor bulk cash transactions conducted with its Mexican (HSBC Mexico) branches and other foreign affiliates and took delivery of more than $15 billion in cash.

    (b) A significant portion of the laundered drug-trafficking proceeds were involved in the Black Market Peso Exchange (BMPE), a complex money laundering system that is designed to move the proceeds from the sale of illegal drugs in the United States to drug cartels outside of the United States, often in Colombia. According to court documents, beginning in 2008, an investigation conducted by the Homeland Security Investigation's El Dorado Task Force, in conjunction with the US Attorney's Office for the Eastern District of New York, identified multiple HSBC Mexico accounts associated with criminal activity and revealed that drug traffickers were depositing hundreds of thousands of dollars in bulk US currency every day into HSBC Mexico accounts. Since 2009, the investigation has resulted in the arrest, extradition, and conviction of numerous individuals illegally using HSBC Mexico accounts in furtherance of criminal activity.[2] These activities resulted in at least $881 million in drug trafficking proceeds — including proceeds of drug trafficking by the Sinaloa Cartel in Mexico and the Norte del Valle Cartel in Colombia — being laundered through HSBC Bank USA. HSBC Group admitted it did not inform HSBC Bank USA of significant AML

---

[2] https://www.justice.gov/opa/pr/hsbc-holdings-plc-and-hsbc-bank-usa-na-admit-anti-money-laundering-and-sanctions-violations.

deficiencies at HSBC Mexico, despite knowing of these problems and their effect on the potential flow of illicit funds through HSBC Bank USA.

3. Ignoring fraudulent activity identified by red flags and helping fraudsters by writing their names in different ways in transactions and payments, including their related parties.

   (a) HSBC removed information identifying the countries from US dollar payment messages by way of deliberately using less-transparent payment messages, known as "cover payments"; and worked with at least one sanctioned entity to fraudulently format payment messages, which helped circumvent the bank's filters from blocking prohibited payments. Specifically, examples of these techniques include:

   i. Inserting cautionary notes in payment messages such as:
      1. "care sanctioned country",
      2. "do not mention our name in NY", or
      3. "do not mention Iran".

Despite the fact that the fine was high compared to previous enforcement actions against banks for compliance control failures, many US Senators (e.g. Elizabeth Warren and Carl Levin), journalists, and concerned citizens raised a concern that such violations are criminal in nature and as such the responsible people should be held accountable for their actions and charged with criminal allegations.

What were the main considerations of the Department of Justice for not subjecting the individuals leading HSBC during the period in which the severe violations took place to criminal proceedings and take the blame for their actions?

The generally accepted reasons are:

- Financial stability — taking extreme actions against the bank, such as revoking its license to do business in the US, would have been a death stroke for HSBC that could have risked financial stability, the financial assets owned by millions of its customers, and the US government could potentially have been asked to back the depositors' assets.
- Loss of jobs for more than 100,000 employee — HSBC is considered an engine of the economy of the City of London, for the number of people who work there.

This case became a case study for many aspects of the fight against financial crimes:

1. The expectation from the banks is much higher than they think — regulators pointed a finger to the bank and its leadership, brought them to admit that by being negligent they were subject to criminal and not only administrative responsibility.
2. The investigations by law enforcement agencies included a deep dive into the bank's information systems — a forensic approach.
3. Banks will need to make sure they have an effective compliance program, such that will pass the investigation test and not just "tick the box".
4. Some may claim that the case demonstrates the opposite — no matter how negligent the bank was, its executives were not exposed to personal liability, and therefore were lacking the motivation to truly take compliance seriously.
5. Governments are taking action related to the HSBC case: for example, two major bills have been introduced in the US Congress:

    a. The Cooperate with Law Enforcement Agencies and Watch Act of 2019 (H.R. 758).

    This bill limits a financial institution's liability for maintaining a customer account or a customer transaction in compliance with a written request by a federal, state, tribal, or local law enforcement agency. A federal or state agency may not take an adverse supervisory action against a financial institution with respect to maintaining an account or a transaction consistent with such a request.

    b. The Corporate Transparency Act (H.R. 2513).

    This would crack down on the illicit use of anonymous shell companies. This bill requires certain new and existing small corporations and limited liability companies to disclose information about their beneficial owners. A beneficial owner is an individual who (1) exercises substantial control over a corporation or limited liability company, (2) owns 25% or more of the interest in a corporation or limited liability company, or (3) receives substantial economic benefits from the assets of a corporation or limited liability company.

Summary

The HSBC case was indeed a critical point that changed the rules of the "game"; large banks understood they can no longer hide behind the same excuses — "we did not know, or senior management was not aware".

Let's think, for a moment, what happened to the financial assets owned by criminals, terrorists, and sanctioned countries that siphoned funds through HSBC, and many other banks, until 2012. It would be a fair estimate to suggest that only a small portion of these funds was confiscated by the law enforcement agencies. What about the funds that were not confiscated? They most likely greased the economy and were mixed in with legitimate activities, served to buy assets, and for the consumption of goods and services.

Governments need to focus on effective measures to stop criminal and terrorism-related activities, and the related financial violations on an on-going basis. Traceability of the funds to the origin is more difficult after long periods of time.

Unfortunately, many white-collar crimes have become entwined in and part of legitimate business activities. Many innocent people were financially involved in the transformation of these assets, making it extremely challenging to separate between legal and illegal money when actions are not taken in a timely manner. Hopefully, the HSBC case has taught us something on how to unwind these activities and allow law enforcement agencies to act swiftly.

Chapter 4

Business Facilitators

Bernard Touboul

For several years now, the public and governments have been increasingly aware of the risks and severity of terrorism and transnational organized crime. Through the use of corruption and money-laundering mechanisms, the illegal economy has deeply infiltrated markets for legitimate goods, services, and financial products worldwide.

Both organized crime and terrorism have expanded exponentially in terms of the number of actors, combatants, victims, and attacks. They have also diversified in influence, legal and illegal financial investments, communications, logistical agility, marketing, and strengthening of their comparative advantages.

In the wake of geopolitical, economic, or societal crises, political and social grievances too often go unanswered by the state. This has then created the critical vacuum sufficient to provide organized crime and terrorism with the opportunity and strength to penetrate states, institutions, and societies and make them fragile, vulnerable, and prey to a widespread sense of insecurity and anxiety. Violence, corruption, and money laundering are the essential vectors that help these harmful organizations succeed.

The fact that criminal syndicates and terrorist organizations are dependent on legitimate business organizations, from giant multinational corporations to retail outlets, is often overlooked. But it must be borne in mind that criminal enterprises are exactly like legal businesses, except that they produce, distribute, and sell illegal products and services. One advantage they have over legitimate businesses is that they do not pay taxes or comply with regulatory restrictions. In illegal markets all social rules are deliberately broken by actors who want to obtain maximum profit regardless of the means used to do so, including violence and corruption and unconcerned with the human and social costs of their acts.

However, even today politicians, law enforcement agencies, judicial systems, and the public at large continue to view them through the emotional lenses of Good and Evil. Strategies to combat crime and terrorism still remain focused on the objectives of seizing or prohibiting illicit goods, products, or money. The decapitation of these harmful organizations through the elimination of the mafia Godfather, terrorist group leader, or criminal gang leader has not yet eradicated illicit or criminal activities. The leaders of the drug cartels in Mexico even manage their international criminal activities from prison. The elimination of Osama bin Laden, the founder of Al Qaeda, and Abu Bakr al-Baghdadi, the head of the Islamic state, has not put an end to the activities of *jihadist* movements or to the lone wolf terrorists in Africa and Europe who still owe allegiance to them. The arrest by the Italian police of Marco Di Lauro in 2019, head of the Neapolitan mafia, has certainly not put an end to the activities of the criminal organizations in Italy, Europe, or the world.

The objectives of the various struggles against crime and terror are narrow. The risk-assessment focuses on the threats of criminal or terrorist attacks and remains partial, without taking into account the investment and organizational strategies of these criminal corporations. The statistics that reflect them are insufficient to understand criminal and terrorist enterprises in their commercial, financial, and highly competitive environments. The criminal organization is permanently exposed to competition. Without possible legal arbitration, in the criminal sphere, the only possible recourse is a matter of both internal and external violence. Consequently, the result of these struggles and efforts remains limited or even insignificant as compared to the growing scale of influence, assets, and incomes from crime and terrorism.

Underlying the objectives of territorial conquest, power, and influence, the rational motivation of profit and money, as a currency of exchange and a vector of power is central to the development, operation, and continued existence of these criminal and terrorist groups in a competitive world of both legal and illegal markets.

The concept of a business model for attacking organized crime and terrorism therefore goes beyond the simple idea that criminals and terrorists need money to launch their attacks.

There is ample evidence that these organizations use business strategies and practices to achieve their criminal objectives.[1] They use the organizational models, structures, and managerial techniques of the business world to penetrate licit and illicit markets. In doing so, they thrive and strive to remain competitive with both other criminal actors as well as legitimate business rivals and competitors. They maintain a sustainable and rational position both within their ideological, religious, or political movements and in the markets and sectors of the crime and terror industries. Today, these organizations are using technological innovations through legal companies and other professional, financial, or non-profit facilitators that allow them to act in an even more discreet, less risky, and more profitable way.

Since the devastating international financial crisis of 2008, globalization has greatly facilitated this growing infiltration of the legitimate world economy by organized crime and terrorist organizations.

The global economy, as it appears today, presents pervasive, structural, and systemic interrelationships between crime, politics, and business. Criminal and terrorist organizations are now functional units of the global economy dominated by the dynamics of competitive markets, the privatization of infrastructure and means of production, and the liberalization of institutional and private financial flows.

In this sense, every enterprise needs other enterprises to carry out its activities. Criminal and terrorist organizations likewise need other enterprises, both legal and illegal, to prosper, maintain a position, diversify their activities, and conceal hidden activities within the flow of international trade and finance. They need legal businesses to surf easily and without limits between the legal and illegal economy, to recycle dirty money, to conceal the nefarious objectives of their legal and illegal activities, and to expand their area of influence and territorial power according to their criminal market shares.

Today, there is an increasing use of these legitimate businesses in illicit markets; this is the cause of the complex and systemic infiltration of

---

[1]Louise I. Shelley, "Dirty Entanglements: Corruption, Crime, and Terrorism", New York, NY: Cambridge University Press, 2014.

crime as well as the structural diversity of economic actors in the global economy.

The number, nature, composition, and level of organization of these entrepreneurial facilitators who assist criminal or terrorist actors vary widely depending on the country, market, opportunity, and the particular stage of the licit and illicit supply chains in which they operate.

This includes fraud schemes with fictitious yet legal companies created in tax havens. It also includes legitimate companies participating in various tax carousels or insurance and bank credit frauds through duly established companies of all sizes (banks, multinationals, SMEs, individual businesses, etc.). Although many criminals today turn to the Internet for the anonymity it offers, the distribution and laundering of stolen and counterfeit products also requires wholesalers and various legitimate businesses to repackage, distribute, store, transport, and sell the products to legitimate customers and institutions such as hospitals and retail outlets. According to an investigation by the National Retail Federation (NRF) in the United States, organized retail crime gangs often use storefronts, pawn shops, flea markets, and kiosks to sell stolen goods. Although crime syndicates have their own assets, they use legitimate commercial transportation, logistics, and distribution companies.[2]

Indeed, once at destination, the trucks or ships must be offloaded, either at the docks or when the trucks reach a storage facility. Then, they must be stored, sometimes in facilities owned by the syndicates, but often in commercial storage facilities. They must be loaded onto trucks or trains for delivery to wholesalers; that is, central distribution points, and from there to retail outlets.

This willing or forced collaboration of many facilitators of criminal and terrorist activities is illustrated by the way the Islamic State (ISIS) financed its barbaric activities while it controlled the oil fields and refineries in areas of Iraq and Syria. Oil companies maintained the refineries in ISIS territory and taught its members to operate them. Truck manufacturers sold tanker trucks to ISIS-controlled buyers. Turkey and various Syrian factions permitted the truck convoys to transit through their territories. Once the trucks reached the ports of Ceyhan in Turkey or Latakia in Syria, the crude oil and products were offloaded onto oil tankers owned by shipping firms. They were then sold to legitimate oil trading

---

[2]NRF web site — "Retailers See Increase in Organized Retail Crime" — https://nrf.com/media-center/press-releases/retailers-see-increase-organized-retail-crime.

companies, which were happy to purchase them, despite knowing exactly where the products came from, because they were able to purchase them at a discount, thus increasing their profit margin when sold into the world market.

It is common nowadays for manufacturers, shipping, transport, and logistics companies, as well as law, financial and accounting, legal, and duly established firms, visible through an official commercial website, to position themselves on the market by openly offering services and products to the detriment of the law and regulations.

In a context where crime is one of the principal driving forces of the world economy, criminals and terrorists have the necessary cash, bank support, and means of coercion to buy and sell at their convenience. The returns on their investments are exorbitant, while the legal global economy is suffering. It is therefore clear that ignoring the criminal nature of the client allows the facilitating businesses to stay in the market and take advantage of it. Thus the use of trade facilitators and legitimate businesses to organize and profit from illicit trade is now widespread.

The facilitation of crime and terrorism by legal business enterprises can indeed be intentional: this is the case of "reverse money laundering", which describes a new form of money laundering. It does not involve income from past crimes, but amounts of clean money to be invested and used to commit future crimes or terrorist attacks (this would be the origin of the funds to commit the 9/11 attack). This may be for ideological reasons, but above all to take advantage of a higher return on investment than investments in the legal financial markets. This is also the case of shell companies in tax havens. The IMF reports that 40% of foreign direct investment worldwide, amounting to $12 trillion, is invested by multinational companies in "shell companies" each year.[3] They offer criminals and terrorists the opportunity to buy legal "ready-made" companies with very lax banking or para-banking conditions and schemes that make it impossible to trace the real owners of the companies and the origin of their resources.

This facilitation can also be unintentional: this is the case of company raids by the mafia,[4] the awarding of public contracts to local SMEs to

---

[3] Damgaardt *et al.*, "Piercing the veil", finance and development — International Monetary Fund, June 2018. The author defines "empty shells" as legally registered companies — usually in a tax haven — but without real economic activity.

[4] Sarah Lain, "Corporate Raiding in Russia: Tackling the Legal, Semi-Legal and Illegal Practices that Constitute Reiderstvo Tactics" RUSI, July 2017.

justify the fraudulent obtaining of public subsidies, the stock market investment through the purchase of shares in legal listed companies, with participation in (or even control of) the boards of directors and their business decision power. Thus, new perspectives are emerging from recent studies and research: the theories of organization and management of legal companies are being applied to the analysis of criminal and terrorist enterprises.

The same principles of corporate strategy, financial management and cost structures, industrial organization, production, value chain and supply chain logistics are being applied. There are also strategies for competition and competitiveness, communication, markets' structure and dynamics, and many others.

Criminal syndicates and terrorist groups can thus run legally established businesses and use the profits to maintain their organizations and illegal activities. Everyone, whether a producer of goods, a service provider, or a business manager, can now be involved (more or less consciously, more or less voluntarily) in both legal, criminal, and terrorist activities. All sectors of economic activity are involved. Anyone can be induced to cooperate with or contribute to the designs of organized crime and terrorist groups. Each may be used (whether unwittingly or not) as part of an agreement or strategic alliance between criminals, terrorists, local politicians, multinational corporations, banks, and professionals, that establishes a mutually profitable division of labor.

For example, this leads to complex patterns of money laundering through the commercial, logistical, and banking operations of legal international trade (trade-based money laundering). It also includes terrorist or criminal groups and networks that use charities or trusts to collect donations from members of the public who support a seemingly charitable cause. New technologies that are legally accessible to all through the Internet allow them to acquire block-chain-based crypto-money for anonymous criminal money transfers and also to exploit social networking platforms for criminal purposes. Finally, all the features and advantages of complex networks are being used to process ever-increasing amounts of criminal transactions while minimizing the risks involved and maximizing profits. Criminal enterprises are now the ones pushing the frontiers of knowledge and innovation. Given the increasing role they play to fill the vacuum in the state, the high profitability, and the limited threat from enforcement authorities, legitimate businesses will undoubtedly become targets more frequently. Paradoxically, today's legal businesses need to learn from criminal and terrorist enterprises how to organize into agile and high-performance networks and profit from some of the global criminals' and gangsters' insights.[5]

Investment in legal businesses is crucial and plays a multifaceted role in the strategies of criminal and terrorist organizations.

As in any business, the revenues generated by the trade in illicit products are used to cover a range of operating expenses; operational, management, personnel, and other costs whose reduction can only improve profits. For example, for the heroin market in Europe, between 25% and 42% of the revenues are ultimately available for investment in the legal economy.[6] This also means that the criminal enterprise, like any legal enterprise, first invests part of its profits in its own business, allowing it to continually improve and expand its operations and diversify its illegal activities according to the opportunities of the moment.

Sectors of activity with the most criminal involvement include: restaurants and bars, transportation and logistics, real estate, hotels, construction, the food supply chain, wholesale and the retail trade in clothing, textiles, and others. Economic activities such as renewable energy, waste and metal management, money transfer activities, gambling, and betting represent a particularly interesting investment potential for these organizations.[7]

Several types of factors determine the attractiveness of criminal investment in legal enterprises. Those that are most popular are generally cash-intensive to facilitate money laundering. Also, those that are labor-intensive, where they can reduce labor costs by exploiting trafficked women and children. An industry's dependence on government administration and public subsidies is a target for criminals and terrorists to corrupt and control the goods and services procurement mechanisms. European agricultural subsidy mechanisms have attracted criminal financial engineering implemented at the expense of European Union finances. This is the example of the control exercised by Italian mafia groups over

---

[5] Marc Goodman, "What Business Can Learn from Organized Crime", *Harvard Business School* (November 2011).

[6] Ernesto U. Savona and Michele Riccardi (eds.), "From Illegal Markets to Legitimate Businesses: The Portfolio of Organized Crime in Europe", Final Report of Project OCP — Organized Crime Portfolio (www.ocportfolio.eu). Trento: Transcrime — Università degli Studi di Trento, 2015.

[7] *Ibid.*

the agri-food industry in Italy; the olive oil sector, dairy products, or organic farming destined for Europe.[8]

Criminal and terrorist organizations will also increasingly target legal businesses that are concentrated in a specific territory in order to take control of it, and markets that are still unregulated, or newly or weakly regulated.

In 2017, the think-tank Global Financial Integrity analyzed 11 major criminal industries worth up to $2.2 trillion[9]: counterfeiting and piracy, drug trafficking, illegal logging, human trafficking, illegal mining, illegal fishing, illegal wildlife trade, crude oil theft, trafficking in small arms and light weapons, illegal trade in organs, and trafficking in cultural property.

Through the hybridization of enterprises that undertake legal, illegal, and even charitable activities, these criminal organizations aim to gain a dominant position in both illegal and legal markets; this requires a permanent concern to maintain perfect control over all kinds of available resources, whatever the means of obtaining them.

The most powerful criminal organizations, such as the Italian or Russian mafias, which compete in volume of sales and net profits with the largest multinationals, are able to control more or less directly whole sections of the economy in their countries of origin or in those where they choose to establish themselves on a long-term basis thanks to complacent, corrupt, or coerced legislators, government officials, bureaucrats, judicial and law-enforcement personnel.

For example, when the financial and banking sector of a fragile state, a tax haven, is under the control of a mafia or a terrorist movement, they are able to use, influence, and infect the global banking and financial system, centered in the City of London, New York, Zurich, Frankfurt, Hong Kong, and others.

The term "economic model" can be applied to organized crime and terrorism to refer to at least three different phenomena:

First, the business model derives from the way criminal and terrorist activities are financed. This corresponds to the type of legal and illegal business sectors and the models from which money and other modes of financing are derived. It is also the type of business models most conducive to criminal and terrorist predators who must ensure

---

[8] Hannah Roberts, "How the Mafia Got to Our Food", *The Financial Times* (November 8, 2018).

[9] https://gfintegrity.org/business-transnational-crime/.

the operational and strategic sustenance of their organizations and members who must prepare and execute their activities.

Secondly, the development of a political economy of terrorism and organized crime seems to be clearly emerging throughout the world. These organizations aim at directing criminal economic activity in the medium and long term, notably through the deep penetration of the legal world economy. They aim to establish and maintain the mafia/ criminal and terrorist economic equilibrium of these organizations through budgetary policies[10], while applying rational models of economic cost and benefit analysis to their crime and terrorist activities. For example, Al Qaeda in Iraq relies, for accounting and financial reasons among others, more on smugglers and criminals than on their own militants to bring recruits to join the *jihad* in Iraq.[11]

Finally, this business model is based on how terrorism is used as a strategy to maintain a status quo (political, societal), where organized crime can more easily thrive and vice-versa; where law enforcement focuses its resources on fighting high-visibility terrorist activities and neglects the opportunistic expansion of criminal gangs into related markets and activities.

Failed states such as Afghanistan, where Al Qaeda and the Taliban are operating, would be an example of this interpretation of terrorism as a business model with a clear strategy of engagement against the United States. For Al Qaeda, this model is based on a competitive and unique positioning strategy within the global *jihadist* movement focused on providing influence, advice, and investment services to the various terrorist groups on the ground. In this context, driven by profit and entrepreneurial success, terrorism is supported not only for ideological reasons but also for both political and economic reasons.

This Al Qaeda business model in Afghanistan is changing. It has evolved from the field of tactical operations to the provision of technical advice, combat training, financial facilitation, communication of local

---

[10]This includes the acquisition of foreign exchange, social assistance — employment, care, education — to populations under influence and control, collection, and tax rates imposed by criminal organizations, and maintenance of criminal governance in controlled territories.

[11]Felter, J. and Fishman, B.: "Al-Qaida's Foreign Fighters in Iraq: A First Look at the Sinjar Records", by Combating Terrorism Center at West Point (January 2008).

jihadist groups and mediation services to non-state supporters or sponsoring states. These services are sold to those whose objectives converge with the ideology of the now criminal-terrorist enterprise[12] that could be named "Al Qaeda Inc". In a strategic approach, Al Qaeda defines its comparative advantage according to a SWOT analysis,[13] to choose and maintain a competitive positioning on which its success and survival depend.

The competition is tough. Islamic state (ISIS), also called "ISIS Inc".[14] in the oil business, with its strong mastery of communication, marketing, and propaganda tools (radicalization, recruitment of *jihadists*, offering a model of society and socio-economic governance based on *Sharia* and misinterpreted Islam). Competition also comes from mafia and criminal organizations that offer access to networks (hawala networks, money-laundering networks, access to companies and off-shore accounts), and to human resources either to facilitate trafficking (drugs, human beings, counterfeiting, cigarettes, weapons…) or to orchestrate hostage-taking, provide smuggling services, and to find clients who buy illicit or stolen products or who would be potential ransom-payers.[15]

The vectors of influence of the criminal and terrorist business are therefore complex and very numerous, due to random and unstable relationships with key strategic partners. These include agreements, alliances, or conflicts with local tribes (as in West Africa and the Sahel), local elected officials and members of corrupt governments or other criminal gangs and terrorist movements. The alliances between Los Zetas in Mexico and Hezbollah or between the FARC in Colombia and Hamas are examples. Also, the hundreds of thousands of refugees who risked their lives to cross the Mediterranean don't pose a threat to Cosa Nostra in

---

[12] Alex Gallo, "Understanding Al Qaida's Business Model", CTC Combating Terrorism Center at West Point, Vol. 4(1), (January 2011).

[13] Michael E Porter, *Competitive Strategy: Techniques for Analyzing Industries and Competitors*, New York, Free Press, 1980 — SWOT (Strengths, Weaknesses, Opportunities, Threats): Model created by Michael Porter to diagnose and define the competitive framework of a company according to internal axes of strengths and weaknesses and external axes of opportunities and threats.

[14] Erika Solomon, Robin Kwong and Steven Bernard, "Inside Isis Inc: The Journey of a Barrel of Oil", *Financial Times* (February 29, 2016).

[15] http://www.ceris.be/fileadmin/library/Research-Papers-Online/Thesis-Deconstructing_the_business_of_terrorism.pdf.

Italy; they even present a brand-new business opportunity. Cosa Nostra, the Sicilian mafia, has implemented a double-dip strategy with African terrorists and criminal gangs. First, the Sicilians force groups like the Nigerian Black Axe gang to buy all of their drugs from them. Then, they collect money for rental of their territory. That way, the Italians can focus on large-scale drug trafficking while still profiting off street sales and at no real risk to themselves since the Black Axe manage the exploitation of new immigrants in distress to do the kind of daily dirty work that carries a high risk of imprisonment. So, the Italian mafia started leaning on the Black Axe and other African criminal and terrorist groups to deal in drugs, even with Italian clients.[16]

Supported by the facilitation of legal but complaisant enterprises, this intersection of criminal, mafia, and terrorist networks is proliferating around the world and can take shape according to three main trends: Coexistence, where these groups occupy and operate in the same geographical space at the same time; and cooperation, where different groups realize that their mutual interests are best served if they work temporarily together and are threatened if they do not. Finally, convergence, when each begins to adopt the behavior that is most often associated with the other.

It is, then, the phenomenon of the gangsterization of terrorism and of the radicalization of gangsters, who find themselves in a common mode of entrepreneurial and managerial operation of their activities.[17]

Case Study

The case of *jihadism* in the Sahel is also illustrative in this sense. Since the 1980s, organized criminal activities have been undertaken by armed groups that have diversified into terrorists, insurgents, criminals, armed defense militias, smugglers, road killers, and local warring tribes that differ according to their vision, mission, and means of action. Building on this context, Al Qaeda's strategic and entrepreneurial organization in the

---

[16]Malia Politzer and Emily Kassie, article in *The Huffington Post*, "The 21st Century Gold Rush How the Refugee Crisis is Changing the World Economy — Part 2: The Mafia Meets the Black Axe", December 2016, https://highline.huffingtonpost.com/articles/en/the-21st-century-gold-rush-refugees/#/niger.
[17]Tawfik Hamel, « DJIHADISME — Le Sahel, où se rencontrent terrorisme et criminalité », *The Maghreb and Orient Courier* (April 2017).

Islamic Maghreb (AQIM) is characteristic of the business model that consolidates the group's specialized activities. In 2013, an Al Qaeda playbook for Mali was uncovered, where the organization's leader, Al-Zawahiri, explained its strategy: establishing unity of efforts (from regional armed groups), mobilizing populations from support in domestic movements to acceptance of global *jihadist* expansionism and cultivation of local support to finally implement the *Sharia*.[18] Thus, AQIM operates in two groups[19]: one in the north of Algeria for operational missions of terrorist attacks, drug distribution in Europe and laundering of criminal proceeds in the real estate market, particularly in the Maghreb. The other in the south of Algeria is active in smuggling, transit of drugs (cocaine) from South America, and also arms, immigrants, cigarettes … through the web of criminal actors and their various fighting motivations orchestrated by Al Qaeda's strategy in West Africa and the Sahel on behalf of the northern organization.

In conclusion, in view of the estimated net profits of the Russian mafia, far exceeding the results of the largest legitimate multinational firms, a Russian policeman interviewed admitted, not without some pride, that "our Vory (Russian mafia) are the best capitalists in the world!"[20]

Therefore, it cannot be sufficiently emphasized that, just as in the case of the professional, financial, NGO, and hi-tech facilitators, the business facilitators of the criminal and terrorist networks are often perfectly aware of whom they are dealing with. In the age of Information, it is better to recognize that ignorance is a choice! There is sometimes coercion, to be sure, particularly when dealing with smaller producers and sellers, but in the majority of cases those who smooth the way for the criminals and terrorists do so out of sheer greed. The criminals have the money that everybody wants — and lots of it!

The legal/illegal hybrid nature of the contemporary world economy is now expressed both at the macroeconomic and microeconomic levels; at the level of the enterprise, the functional unit of the capitalist and liberal market system, the essential objective of which is profit. With similar

---

[18] Jami Forbes, article: "Revisiting the Mali al-Qaida Playbook: How the Group is Advancing on its Goals in the Sahel", CTC Combating Terrorism Center at West Point. Vol. 11(9), (October 2018).

[19] *Ibid.*

[20] Mark Galeotti, *The Vory: Russia's Super Mafia*, Yale University Press, New Haven, p. 203, (May 2018).

managerial strategies, criminal enterprises cooperate, converge, compete, and position their "brand"; threaten but also use and trade with legal enterprises of all kinds and sizes, as well as with other criminal enterprises and terrorists.

In the context of widespread global corruption where money laundering is a key driver of the global economy, the state, in its governance role, is no longer able (maybe not even willing) to eradicate organized crime and terrorism. In this complex environment, legal economic actors face a dilemma. They cannot be ignorant of or absent from the illicit markets, otherwise they would not be able to remain competitive or even survive the dynamics of lucrative legal markets. Criminal "demand" today exceeds legitimate and regulated "supply". If these actors refuse to buy from or sell to criminal enterprises, it is certain that a competitor, whether in the developed or developing world, whether legal or illegal, will do so. This is the case for financial institutions, banks, multinational firms, SMEs, service providers (lawyers, accountants, business consultants, grocers, or pizza makers…) as well as producers of all kinds of goods at risk, in any case, of counterfeiting.

Money is money; it is not clean or dirty, it is simply money, meaning it can be both or either — and everyone in business has to do business and make money … or wither and die!

Chapter 5

Non-Profit Facilitators

Rachel Ehrenfeld

The rapidly increasing role of domestic advocacy groups, known as non-governmental organizations (NGOs),[1] and of International NGOs (INGOs)[2] have been a matter of concern for a long time.

NGOs did not exist until 1945, when they were created to help rebuild the world after the Second World War ended. The Encyclopedia Britannica[3] defines an NGO as a "voluntary group of individuals or organizations, usually not affiliated[4] with any government, that is formed to provide services or to advocate a public policy. NGOs may be financed by private donations, international organizations, governments, or a combination of these". These post-WWII NGOs have joined thousands of existing "charitable" non-profits that already existed. Many Islamic NGOs, for example, advocate changing Western legal systems in accordance with *Sharia* law, especially in Europe and the US, where they regularly work in tandem with radical Left groups.

As of this writing, there are 197 countries in the world and 10 million NGOs[5] worldwide (!) Many of them operate in collaboration with tens of

---

[1] https://en.wikipedia.org/wiki/Non-governmental_organization.

[2] https://www.amazon.com/NGOs-International-Politics-Shamima-Ahmed/dp/1565492307.

[3] https://www.britannica.com/topic/nongovernmental-organization.

[4] https://www.merriam-webster.com/dictionary/affiliated.

[5] http://www.theglobaljournal.net/.

thousands of INGOs. (Last available data from 2013, said there were more than 40,000 INGOs.[6])

It is important to note that "INGOs are not elected bodies, are not founded on the principle of representation, and are not accountable to the public", as pointed[7] out by Dr. Raphael Ben-Ari, an expert on NGOs and international law. INGOs have no legal recognition and guidelines, and some are known for regularly publishing biased "fact-finding" reports that are rarely questioned by the media or even "national courts and international tribunals and institutions".[8]

NGOs and the INGOs that often fund them claim to advance civil society, democracy, education, free speech, justice reform, public health, and protect human rights, environmentalism, and similar noble causes. Funding for such groups comes from wealthy individuals, charities, inter-governmental organizations, international organizations, and also from national wealth funds, and individual governments that use the NGOs and INGOs as proxies to extend their policies and interests. Anyone can establish a domestic NGO, in compliance with the local laws. An INGO can also be established by anyone, "… and start issuing human rights fact-finding reports that would then be relied on by the media, or worse — by national courts and international tribunals".[9] However, the wealthier the INGO, the greater its influence.

Unfortunately, in many instances, the NGOs/INGOs' activities are divorced from their mission statements. Moreover, they can be easily manipulated by terrorist and criminal groups to mask their activities.

Global Islamic charities have often masked their funding of the propagation of radical Islamic ideology under the guise of support of education, health, and economic development. Large Islamic NGOs/INGOs often operate as extensions of Muslim governments, such as Saudi Arabia, Qatar, Iran, and Turkey. In addition to assisting Muslim communities in need, they have also funded Islamic terrorist groups, such as Al Qaeda, Hamas, the Palestinian Islamic *Jihad*, Hezbollah, and the Muslim Brotherhood, to name a few.

---

[6] https://jcpa.org/article/international-nongovernmental-organizations-global-conscience-or-powerful-political-actors/.

[7] *Ibid.*

[8] *Ibid.*

[9] *Ibid.*

Here are a few examples:

Investigations into Al Qaeda's attacks on the United States and other radical Muslim terrorist attacks in Europe and elsewhere, have, for example, helped to lift the veil from the Saudi-based charity/INGO, the International Islamic Relief Organization (IIRO), exposing its funding of Al Qaeda.

The IIRO was implicated in funding the 1993 World Trade Center bombing, as well as the 1998 bombing of the US embassies in Kenya and Tanzania. The IIRO denied any involvement with Al Qaeda. But after the FBI raided the IIRO offices in Virginia, they were shut down in March 2002.[10] Other Al Qaeda linked NGOs have also been shut down in the US and elsewhere.

Tracing the origins and the operations of global Islamic INGOs can be complicated. A good example is the Vienna, Austria-based NGO, the "Third World Relief Agency" (TWRA),[11] billed as a "humanitarian organization". It was founded by the Sudanese Muslim Brother Elfatih Hassanein, funded by the Sultan of Brunei, the Saudi Royal Family, and Iran, and "run by senior Bosnian government officials".

According to J. Millard Burr,[12] "While carrying out some legitimate humanitarian functions as a cover, the TWRA was a front for global terrorist operations. By the early nineteen-nineties it became the chief broker of Balkan black-market weapons deals. It was directly involved in the funding and movement of arms from Sudan to Croatia and other locations in the Balkans. It opened offices in Bosnia, Turkey, and Russia and used accounts in Liechtenstein and Monaco to launder the funds it received. Some $80 million were remitted from a Vienna account in the First Austrian Bank in 1992, followed by $231 million in 1993, the highpoint in its operation". It later moved from Austria to Turkey.

The German intelligence[13] services identified transfers of hundreds of millions of dollars from TWRA to fund the relocation of hundreds,

---

[10] https://www.amazon.com/Funding-Evil-Updated-Terrorism-Financed/dp/1566252318.
[11] https://acdemocracy.org/al-qaedas-balkan-ties-the-bosnian-connections-to-the-world-trade-center-attacks-an-acd-exclusive/.
[12] https://acdemocracy.org/the-islamist-dominance-in-turkey-part-i.
[13] https://www.globalmbwatch.com/2009/06/25/us-muslim-brotherhood-funded-islamist-arms-network-in-early-1990s/.

if not thousands, of Afghan *jihadis* and Al Qaeda members to fight in Bosnia in the 1990s.[14]

Another report, by the Central Intelligence Agency (CIA)[15] in 1996, found that "more than 50 Islamic non-governmental organizations (NGOs) operated in Bosnia". Most had Saudi funding and supported terrorist groups or employed individuals suspected of having terrorist connections".

For many years, the major supporter of Palestinian terrorist organization Hamas was the Texas-based Holy Land Foundation for Relief and Development (HLF),[16] which operated as an NGO in the US. Hamas was designated as a terrorist organization by the US government in 1995, but that did not stop the HLF from transferring more than $12.4 million to Hamas through its branches in the West Bank and Gaza, "… to support schools that served Hamas's ends by encouraging children to become suicide bombers[17] and to recruit suicide bombers by offering support to their families". The HLF was designated by The US Treasury Department as a "Specially Designated Terrorist" group and shut down in December 2001.[18]

A long list detailing information about US-based charities/NGOs that funded Palestinian and other Islamic terrorist groups is available on a special US Treasury Department's website.[19]

Many pro-Palestinian NGOs and INGOs that operate today in the US, as well as other Western nations, are funding, directly and indirectly, so-called Palestinian "human rights" organizations that together with the BDS movement advocate against the State of Israel, calling for its destruction. They organize demonstrations, hold conferences and "resistance" training courses, file imaginary "hate" and frivolous discrimination lawsuits, as part of their lawfare that aims to bring the American companies down (not individuals, only companies from which large amounts of money can be extorted). The Atlanta-based EPPS Aviation[20] is one of very few companies that fought back and won.[21]

---

[14] *Ibid.*

[15] https://www.wsj.com/articles/SB10524385762417300.

[16] https://en.wikipedia.org/wiki/Holy_Land_Foundation_for_Relief_and_Development.

[17] https://en.wikipedia.org/wiki/Suicide_bomber.

[18] https://archives.fbi.gov/archives/news/stories/2008/november/hlf112508.

[19] https://www.treasury.gov/resource-center/terrorist-illicit-finance/Pages/protecting-charities_execorder_13224-e.aspx.

[20] http://eppsaviation.com/.

[21] https://acdemocracy.org/epps-aviation-vs-hijab/.

The Islamic NGO that leads these frivolous lawsuits in the US is the Muslim Brotherhood-affiliated Council on American-Islamic Relations (CAIR),[22] which was also named as an unindicted co-conspirator with the HLF. Such organizations should have had their tax exemption removed a long time ago. However, political considerations and "political correctness" seem to have been at work, and certain Islamic charities/NGOs and INGOs have been free to advance their agenda, which is often supported by "progressive" Left-leaning organizations.

Case Study: Open Society Foundations (OSF)

A central element of the Palestinians'' effort to delegitimize the Jewish State of Israel is their international campaign of Boycott, Divestment, and Sanctions against Israel. The BDS[23] movement planned and organized its international campaign in collaboration with "a network of closely linked NGOs (national Non-Governmental Organizations), which are conducting anti-Israel activities".[24]

Billionaire George Soros's Open Society Foundations (OSF),[25] is but one example. The OSF, Soros's flagship charity[26] operates as an International Non-Governmental Organization (INGO). It boasts on its website that Soros is "the world's largest private funder of independent groups working for justice, democratic governance, and human rights", and "is the largest private charity in the world". OSF's budget for 2020 is said to be $1.2 billion.[27]

Soros's private INGO exponentially grows its network of thousands of local and multi-national NGO's. OSF's Left-leaning political preferences dictate their linked NGOs' activities, and creates short and long-term aggregate influence that misleads the public and often corrupts national and international institutions. A recent study by the European Centre for Law and Justice,[28] which exposed that a large number of the

---

[22] https://www.investigativeproject.org/1854/doj-cairs-unindicted-co-conspirator-status-legit.
[23] https://bdsmovement.net.
[24] https://www.gov.il/en/Departments/General/terrorists_in_suits.
[25] https://www.opensocietyfoundations.org/who-we-a.
[26] Soros and his family members operate other charities outside the OSF umbrella.
[27] https://www.opensocietyfoundations.org/.
[28] https://eclj.org.

"judges working for the European Court of Human Rights (ECHR) were, at some point in the past, working for George Soros's Open Society Foundation (OSF) or related NGOs".[29]

The OSF's network supports the Palestinian, anti-Israeli plan in general, as well as direct and indirect funding of organizations affiliated with the BDS movement, thus offering them the facade of legitimacy.

As George Soros tells it, he established his charities purportedly to promote his vision of an "Open Society". The OSF's mission statement[30] affirms it provides grants for political advocacy to fulfill and promote Soros's vision of an open society. Today, OSF's political activism extends to more than 120 countries, where it has distributed more than "50,000 grants", to local NGOs and individuals who claim to be independent and sometimes even non-partisan. Yet they are tasked to "promote" Soros's and the OSF's "values".[31]

Soros's generous funding and international network of politicians, institutions, and the Left-leaning media provides him a huge influence on national and international politics.

Soros is free to spend his money as he pleases. But he should not mask his activities under the fictional veil of "charity". The US Internal Revenue Service (IRS) should have stopped Soros from using the OSF's non-profit status to conduct political indoctrination and instigate revolutionary policies that, while not always successful, cause social, economic, and political upheaval.

The US Internal Revenue code 501(c)(3)[32] stipulates that non-profit organizations are prohibited from "supporting or opposing the election of a candidate for public office at the federal, state, or local level ... and is cause for loss of tax-exempt status. Prohibited activities include endorsement, cash or in-kind contributions (including publicity, staff time, and use of facilities or assets such as photocopiers) to candidates or political parties, working for or against a candidate, rating or evaluating candidates, and coordinating activities with organizations having political

---

[29] https://gript.ie/report-soros-funded-ngos-undermine-independence-of-european-court-human-rights/.

[30] https://www.opensocietyfoundations.org/about/mission-values.

[31] https://www.opensocietyfoundations.org/.

[32] https://ww1.insightcced.org/uploads/publications/legal/lobbying_outline_political_activity.pdf.

aims (such as campaign committees, PACs, and Section 501(c)(4) organizations).

1. A Section 501(c)(3) organization cannot set up, fund, or manage a Political Action Committee (PAC). PACs are special funds set up under Section 527. PACs that support federal candidates are subject to federal campaign finance rules and Federal Election Commission oversight.
2. A Section 501(c)(3) organization can engage in certain voter education activities without loss of tax-exempt status. Special, additional restrictions apply to private foundations (not discussed here)".[33]

The regulations clarify that "no substantial part of the activities involve carrying on propaganda, or otherwise attempting, to influence legislation, or promoting political candidates. It does not qualify as a charity — on a level with building homeless shelters, hospitals, schools, feeding the hungry, etc. Moreover, according to Transparify[34] — the only global transparency rating group for Think-Tanks surveyed the major "200 think-tanks in 47 countries worldwide. "Their 2016 analysis rated "Soros's Open Society Foundations (OSF) as "highly opaque",[35] with the rating of "0". "Additionally, it was the only think-tank in the United States to score so low".[36] Yet, the OSF still operates as a charity that sometimes disburses funding from the US government, the EU and other international bodies, often without acknowledging such collaboration.

Soros's OSF calls for and funds NGOs and individuals for training to organize protests and large-scale demonstrations and teaching resistance techniques. They also call for and support activities against nationalism, Judeo-Christian values and traditions, and Capitalism. Soros's foundations also support fighting against global warming, and for "global social

---

[33] *Ibid.*

[34] http://static1.squarespace.com/static/52e1f399e4b06a94c0cdaa41/t/5773022de6f2e1ecf70b26d1/1467154992324/Transparify+2016+Think+Tanks+Report.pdf.

[35] https://dailycaller.com/2016/07/06/george-soros-open-society-foundations-named-2016s-least-transparent-think-tank/.

[36] See footnote 34.

justice" and transgenderism, population control, and free abortion, to mention but a few.

The billions Soros spent has already made deep inroads into pre-disposed academic institutions and led to significant modifications in our social discourse and political conventions. If the past is of any indication, and with billions more left to his OSF, Soros's radical socialist legacy is likely to continue fueling political, economic, and social turmoil.

Soros seems to have developed a distinct disdain for the Jewish State of Israel. For he has rewritten Middle Eastern history to better coincide with his idea of the "poignant and difficult case" of "victims turning per-petrators". Soros, much like the virulent anti-Semitic graphic daily propa-ganda in Arab, Palestinian, and Iranian newspapers, has been comparing Israel's self-defense against repeated attempts of annihilation by the Islamist/Arab terrorists to Nazi atrocities. The successful defense against Terrorism by preemptive actions is never appropriate in Soros's book.

Noam Chomsky or Yasser Arafat could have written Soros's version of how Israel fought for its independence. "After the war [World War II], Jews resorted to terrorism against the British in Palestine in order to secure a homeland in Israel", Soros writes in his book, *The Bubble of American Supremacy.*[37] "Subsequently, after being attacked by Arab nations, Israel occupied additional territory and expelled many of the inhabitants. Eventually, the Arab victims also turned perpetrators, and Israel started suffering terrorist attacks".

This interpretation of Soros denies the number of Arab invasions and the brutal tactics used that led Israel to occupy the lands from where these attacks were launched. And as for the "expulsions", most left of their own accord because the surrounding Arab nations ordered them to leave. The Arab plan was to kill all the Jews as soon as possible and move back. For defending themselves, the Jews are getting what they deserve in Soros's mind. By surviving Arab/Muslim violence all these years, and by defending themselves, the Jews in Israel and elsewhere bear the responsi-bility for rising anti-Semitism and anti-Israel activities.

In November 2003, as Operation Iraqi Freedom was underway and anti-American and anti-Israeli/anti-Semitic demonstrations spread throughout Europe, Soros appeared for the first time at a meeting of

---

[37] https://www.amazon.com/Bubble-American-Supremacy-Costs-Bushs/dp/B0007XWNFA.

the Jewish Funders Network in New York. He made these remarks: "The policies of the Bush administration and the Sharon administration contribute" to the rise of anti-Semitism.[38] He assured his audience that once Bush and Sharon are removed from office, the world will go back to not hating Jews. "If we change that direction, then anti-Semitism also will diminish. I can't see how one could confront it directly", he said. The vast and sharp denouncement of Soros's statements' as "biased, bigoted [and] absolutely obscene",[39] did not affect his determination to "hold Israel accountable",[40] as displayed in the leaked 2016 Open Society Foundations (OSF) documents.

The 2016 D.C. Leaks revealed[41] that OSF's "progressive national security policies" included plans to "hold Israel accountable" for alleged breaches of international law. This plan entailed generous donations to Palestinian and pro-Palestinian, anti-Zionist Israeli, and Arab "human rights" NGOs in Israel, which aim to undermine the country's democracy within, and lobbies the US Congress, the European Parliament, the United Nations, and other international and foreign governments and organizations and media in efforts to delegitimize the Jewish State of Israel.

From 2001 to 2015, OSF and other Soros-related foundations funneled[42] nearly $10 million to various liberal Jewish and Palestinian groups to intensify anti-Israel propaganda. In 2010, for example, the OSF pledged $100 million[43] over ten years to Human Rights Watch (HRW),[44] whose funding was dwindling following its Saudi fund-raising in 2009. The HRW is a powerful organization that, for decades, has been promoting the Palestinian cause, including support of the BDS, while demonizing Israel.[45]

---

[38] http://www.urielheilman.com/soros.html.

[39] *Ibid.*

[40] https://www.bloomberg.com/view/articles/2016-08-16/how-george-soros-threatens-to-make-israel-a-pariah.

[41] *Ibid.*

[42] https://www.algemeiner.com/2016/09/28/george-soros-israel-hatred-spills-out-into-the-open/.

[43] https://www.hrw.org/news/2010/09/07/george-soros-give-100-million-human-rights-watch.

[44] http://www.hrw.org/.

[45] https://www.ngo-monitor.org/ngos/human_rights_watch_hrw_/.

The OSF[46] network has also been funding organizations known for supporting the Boycott, Divestment, and Sanctions (BDS) movement,[47] including virulent anti-Israel, pro-BDS individuals, and groups affiliated with known Palestinian terrorist groups, especially the Popular Front for the Liberation of Palestine (PFLP).[48] The Israeli government's February 2019 report, *Terrorists in Suit*[49], provides detailed information on "The ties between NGOs promoting BDS and terror organizations". (Additional information is available on the website of NGO Monitor).[50]

Expert testimony before Congress in 2017[51] has documented that one of the oldest Palestinian terror organizations controls important elements of the international operations of the unincorporated entity (the BDS movement) under which the US Domestic Terror Affiliates operate.

OSF's Terrorist Linked Funding: A Few Examples

The Gaza-based NGO, Palestinian Centre for Human Rights (PCHR),[52] claims to be "Dedicated to protecting human rights, promoting the rule of law, and upholding democratic principles in the Occupied Palestinian Territories". In reality, the PCHR is a major actor in the Palestinian efforts to delegitimize Israel, employing disinformation and Lawfare to "galvanize international pressure and punitive measures against Israel in the legal realm". The PCHR "has multiple links" to the Popular Front for the Liberation of Palestine (PFLP),[53] a terrorist organization designated as such by the US, EU, Canada, and Israel. The PCHR's 2017 annual report[54] lists Open Society Foundation as a contributor. However, the amount was not disclosed.

---

[46] https://www.ngo-monitor.org/funder/open_society_institute_osi_/.
[47] https://www.gov.il/BlobFolder/generalpage/terrorists_in_suits/en/De-Legitimization%20Brochure.pdf.
[48] https://www.ngo-monitor.org/topics/popular-front-for-the-liberation-of-palestine-pflp/.
[49] See footnote 47.
[50] https://www.ngo-monitor.org/.
[51] http://docs.house.gov/meetings/FA/FA13/20170202/105508/HHRG-115-FA13- Wstate-SchanzerJ-20170202.pdf.
[52] http://pchrgaza.org/en/.
[53] https://www.ngo-monitor.org/topics/popular-front-for-the-liberation-of-palestine-pflp/.
[54] https://pchrgaza.org/en/wp-content/uploads/2018/06/annual-report-english2017.pdf#page=4.

Adalah,[55] the "Palestinian Arab-run"[56] Israel-based NGO, and the Palestinian NGO Al-Haq,[57] that are linked with the PFLP, also received funding from OSF. Despite mountains of evidence, OSF did not stop funding these and similar groups.

According to the OSF's grant database in 2011 and 2012, the organization gave Al-Haq $100,000 each year.[58] In 2014, Al-Haq received $309,000 from OSF, $400,00 in 2016, and two grants totaling $891,630 in 2017. OSF awarded Adalah NIS756,000 in 2015, and $400,000 in 2017.[59]

OSF has been denying supporting BDS groups directly or indirectly.

Adalah established branches in the US through the "Adalah Justice Project (AJP)[60] with offices in Illinois, Boston, and New York. According to NGO Monitor[61]: "Adalah is a member of the UN-OCHA", the Legal Task Force led by the Norwegian Refugee Council (NRC).[62] The task force coordinates legal responses by 14 Palestinian, Israeli, and international NGOs, including those with ties to the Popular Front for the Liberation of Palestine.

In addition to direct funding, the OSF and other Soros-related charities frequently use Tides Center,[63] which serves as a distribution center for a large number of foundations. In 2016, for example, Tides received $4.53 million[64] from George Soros's foundation to Promote Open Society, which is run by Alexander Soros. "Tides Foundation and Tides Foundation and its offshoot, the Tides Center, are "public charities", which, through donor-advised giving, act as a fiscal sponsor to smaller charities". According to Center for Organizational Research and Education (CORE),[65] Tides created "a model for grantmaking — one that strains the boundaries of US tax law in the pursuit of its leftist, activist goals. This pass-through funding vehicle provides public-relations insulation for the money's

[55] https://www.adalah.org/en/content/view/7189.

[56] *Ibid.*

[57] http://www.ngo-monitor.org/ngos/al_haq/.

[58] https://www.opensocietyfoundations.org/grants/past?filter_keyword=al-Haq.

[59] http://www.ngo-monitor.org/funder/open_society_institute_osi_/.

[60] https://www.adalahjusticeproject.org/.

[61] https://www.ngo-monitor.org/ngos/adalah/.

[62] https://www.ngo-monitor.org/funder/norwegian_refugee_council_/.

[63] https://www.tides.org/impact-partners/explore-our-partners/.

[64] https://www.influencewatch.org/person/george-soros/.

[65] https://www.activistfacts.com/about/.

original donors. By using Tides to funnel its capital, a large public charity can indirectly fund a project with which it would prefer not to be directly identified in public".[66]

Tides regularly passes funds from Soros's various foundations, not only to organizations promoting progressive/socialist causes in the US but also to groups, such as Dream Defenders,[67] "which carries a Tides Foundation logo on its website".[68]

Dream Defenders was "initially formed to protest "Stand-your-ground laws", in 2012 in Florida". Soon after, it was "repurposed to serve the anti-Israel BDS movement". Dream Defenders openly "supports and promotes the mission of the Popular Front for the Liberation of Palestine (PFLP), a US-designated terror organization. The PFLP has used bombings, shootings, and plane hijackings to achieve its political goals".[69]

Yet, Dream Defenders and its members endorsed the PFLP and espoused its tactics by backing PFLP terrorists on social media and at various public events. It brings people to the Middle East to meet with PFLP members and PFLP-affiliated organizations. In March 2016, Dream Defenders put together an alternative school curriculum that includes the PFLP as one of nine "heroes" that should be used to teach "rebellion" strategies and tactics.

The group identifies with the PFLP's struggle, stating: "They [the PFLP] want to be free from global imperialism. They want liberation. They want equal rights. Just like the Dream Defenders".

Adalah,[70] an Israel-based NGO, with branches in the US conducts "legal warfare (Lawfare) campaigns against Israel in international courts and other legal forums, presents Israel as a racist and undemocratic state",[71] and has working relations with the PFLP,[72] a regular recipient of OSF grants, supports the AJP, with mostly undisclosed funds. Another major US charity, which also supports many Palestinian groups, including

---

[66] https://www.activistfacts.com/?s=Tides.

[67] https://jcpa.org/article/american-non-government-organizations-are-intertwined-with-pflp-terror-group/.

[68] http://dreamdefenders.org/staff/.

[69] https://legalinsurrection.com/2016/10/dream-defenders-defending-the-dream-of-anti-israel-activism/.

[70] See footnote 61.

[71] *Ibid.*

[72] *Ibid.*

BDS activists with ties to the PFLP, is the Rockefeller Brothers Fund,[73] which in June 2018 authorized Tides Center to give a $160,000 grant to AJP.[74]

Dream Defenders', Al Haq's, The Palestinian Center for Human Rights', and Adalah's anti-Israel activities are no secret. They have been publicizing them for years. And the OSF often hypes these groups on its "Grantee Spotlight" page.[75]

OSF willfully disregards the evidence that these groups not only promote the BDS but also have close ties to the PFLP, Hamas,[76] and the Palestinian Islamic *Jihad* (PIJ)[77] — all US designated terrorist groups.

Soros's spokesperson Michael Vachon made a feeble attempt of plausible deniability in April 2019. While denying Soros's organizations' support of BDS groups, Vachon admitted that at times they simply don't know how their support is being used. "The foundation cannot track every project connected to every organization that it has supported over the decades", he stated.[78]

OSF's flagrant funding of groups known for their advancement of the Palestinian agenda, and collaboration with Palestinian terrorist groups and individuals, shows that the OSF and other Soros-linked organizations used to indirectly fund terror affiliated groups are ignoring their fiduciary responsibility. Since financial assets are fungible, and BDS groups with links to the PFLP are known to collaborate both formally and informally, all contributions could be laundering money, all violating US laws banning support of terrorists directly and in kind.

Indifference is not a defense for financing Terrorism. It's time the OSF, Soros, their affiliated NGOs and INGOs are held accountable.

---

[73] https://www.ngo-monitor.org.il/funder/rbf/.

[74] https://www.rbf.org/grantees/tides-center.

[75] https://www.opensocietyfoundations.org/voices?page=1&f%5b0%5d=field_taxonomy_regions%3A35.

[76] https://www.terrorism-info.org.il/en/?s=HAMAS.

[77] https://www.terrorism-info.org.il/en/?s=PIJ.

[78] https://momentmag.com/soros-a-small-sacrifice-for-netanyahu/.

https://doi.org/10.1142/9789811229138_0006

Chapter 6

Hi-Tech Facilitators

Bernard Touboul

Actors in cyberspace help criminals and terrorists to achieve their evil purposes. This is a new dimension to the traditional criminal activities, such as buying and selling illicit products, child pornography, and all the rest, which existed before the digital world, continue to exist in the traditional crime world, and are today also practiced through computers, the Internet, and social networks.

Through several examples of illicit trade, frauds, and crimes, this chapter illustrates the development of the conditions for facilitating crime through the misuse of computers, the Internet, telecommunications, and social networks. This new cyber dimension has changed the nature, scale, and spread of crime and terrorism.

Without effective protection against this cyber domain, the vulnerability of states and their institutions, businesses and networks, society, and individuals, to organized crime and terrorism could become irreversible, offering the most fragile option that of tolerating the situation or even capitulating.

Cyberspace is often defined as the interaction of the real and the virtual,[1] the promise of a better future and at the same time the area of greatest risks and the most frightening threats to humanity. Its duality is the result of a revolution that is primarily technological but also cultural.

---

[1] Alix Desforges, article « Les représentations du cyberespace: un outil géopolitique » in Hérodote 2014/1–2 (n° 152–153), pp. 67–81.

Technological advances since Gutenberg have always been aimed at improving the human condition to the point of becoming synonymous with progress in Western thought. In the same way that we used to refer to priests in the Middle Ages, today we blindly abandon ourselves into the hands of scientists and technologists to solve our problems and improve our living conditions. The belief is that nothing can now justify questioning economic and political models based on scientific rationalism since only science and technology guarantee the well-being of individuals and societies.

Today, thousands of satellites revolve around the Earth. Every day, more and more secrets about the structure of the material world are being revealed and open the way to new inventions with their direct and daily applications to our lives.

The economic and political stakes of the new technologies have become extremely important. Power has evolved from tool making in the Stone Age to mastering cyberspace in our information age. Access to finance, research, the development of infrastructure and equipment, and the industrialization of applied sciences are helping to define our structure of life and our way of thinking.

Belief in rational and objective science leads us to interpret our complex environment and respond to it according to the very laws that this belief imposes. Belief can only confirm itself. Therefore, it is not surprising that the hyper-scientific and technological cyberspace that transcends the earthly reality of humans has become the inevitable future of mankind. Only a paradigm shift from blind trust in science and technology can bring about new, more encompassing beliefs, that are more relevant for explaining and living in the contemporary world.[2]

The end of the 20th century saw the emergence of our techno-society whose culture is associated with new information and communication technologies. Already in 1948, Norbert Wiener, the founder of cybernetics and a mathematician, developed the idea that information and communication are essential to the development and functioning of society.[3]

---

[2] Thomas S. Kuhn, *The Structure of Scientific Revolutions,* Chicago: University of Chicago Press (1970).

[3] Norbert Wiener, "Cybernetics: Or Control and Communication in the Animal and the Machine". Paris (Hermann & Cie) & Camb. Mass. (MIT Press) — 1948, 2nd Revised Ed. 1961.

Thus, even before the advent of the Internet, communication and information became liberating for the individual, the state, and society. Democracy is legitimized by science and technology. The social networks supported by the Internet strengthen its representativeness every day. The digital world is also the world of media, the world of information from and for the public with the modern communication technologies.[4]

Human activity is taking on a new dimension which is no longer merely terrestrial but cosmic and spatial. Technological revolutions have followed one after another. Steam has mechanized production. Electricity has created the conditions for mass production. The revolution in electronics and information technology has made it possible to automate production, distribution, and management. Since the end of the 20th century, the merging of different technologies has, at an exponential rate, blurred the boundaries between the physical, the digital, and the biological spheres. This upheaval is affecting the way we live, work, and interact socially. These profound changes have metamorphosed entire systems of production, management, and, above all, governance.

Billions of people are interconnected by mobile devices, in networks allowing unlimited access to information (and disinformation) about everything and everyone in a ubiquity still difficult to imagine. All these possibilities open up new avenues for progress and science. Then, the advent of emerging cutting-edge technologies came in the fields of robotics, artificial intelligence, the Internet of Things, nanotechnologies, biotechnologies, cognitive sciences, energy storage, quantum computing, and others.

The very definition of Man is evolving. The mind, if not the brain of the new generations, develops and vibrates at the dimension and rhythm of a timeless and cosmic access to information. Digital technology has reduced both time and space.[5] There are no fixed locations or coordinates of the events of cyberspace, which is in constant movement and transformation at the speed of light. Data, information, and money now travel around the world almost instantaneously. A subculture of techno-society

---

[4] Christian Aghroum, « cyberterrorisme et sécurité des entreprises » in Cairn. Info-« Sécurité et stratégie » (April 28, 2017), pp. 46–51, https://www.cairn.info/revue-securite-et-strategie-2017-4-page-46.htm.

[5] Stephen, D. McDowell, P. E. Steinberg and Tami K. Tomasello, *Managing the Infosphere: Governance, Technology, and Cultural Practice in Motion*, Temple University Press (2008).

has developed to associate everyday reality with representations of humanity (mankind seeking knowledge and control of the cosmos), and also with those of technology, science fiction, personal development, and the cosmos.

Cyberspace merges reality with the virtual and the imaginary. It represents a dematerialized, borderless, anonymous space, a window of freedom, sharing, and communication.[6] It is a meeting point between the real and the invisible. But it is also the place from which crime intensifies its effects, extends its impact, and accelerates its virality. The place where crime becomes as fast as the flow of electrons, while the police still only act at the pace of the law, and state justice is only applied at the pace of its bureaucracy. The Internet has emerged as a key facilitator for organized crime according to Europol.[7]

Cyberspace is a vector of democracy and at the same time a factor in facilitating and developing crime and terrorism. It is the driving force of a growing democracy in the world, a pillar in the construction of developing, transitional, or emerging States, a libertarian vector of progress and peace. But it is also the instrument of the Big Brother state with unprecedented control over populations, their influence, and manipulation. For example, the digital tool TOR (The Onion Routing) is the result of technological innovation.[8] It creates layers of computer security that prevent computer data from being traced back to its origin. It allows democratic journalists and citizens in revolt to reveal and share with the world information about the realities of a closed dictatorial and authoritarian regime. However, it also makes it possible to hide and anonymize the origin of a criminal site on the Dark Web or to encrypt exchanges during a criminal transaction. Malware (like Flame) can even be programed to "disappear without leaving a trace".[9]

---

[6] Alix Desforges, article « Les représentations du cyberespace: un outil géopolitique » dans Hérodote 2014/1–2 (n° 152–153), pp. 67–81.

[7] Europol — Organised Crime Threat Assessment Report 2011. In its report of 2017, Europol mentions that "the use of new technologies by organized crime groups (OCGs) has an impact on criminal activities across the spectrum of serious and organized crime. This includes developments online, such as the expansion of online trade and widespread availability of encrypted communication channels".

[8] Xavier Raufer, "Cyber-Criminologie", Ed. CNRS, p. 123.

[9] Information Report No. 681 from the French Senate, about the Cyber Defense, by M. Jean-Marie Bockel, Senator, p. 17.

Finally, cyberspace is the place where the paths of crime converge, blurring the traditional distinctions between cyber-violation, fraud, and traditional crime. It is the space where the criminal offenses of corruption, kidnapping for ransom, illicit trafficking in goods and persons, or financial fraud, which already existed, find an additional dimension. Crime has a changing nature that law enforcement and the judiciary find difficult to grasp, especially in the framework of the Westphalian state and the traditionally-defined rule of law.

Initially, the cyber-offender's only ambition, in a libertarian spirit, is to show off his or her technical skills, to demonstrate the ability to trick a computer and computer systems or to expose their flaws. They often view the Internet as public space for everyone and do not see their actions as criminal! In cyberspace, total freedom, implying the feeling that "everything is allowed to me, nothing can stop me and nobody will know it is me", is finally an accessible reality. Offenders may do this for a variety of reasons: recognition of their technological prowess by their peers in the cyber world, retaliation by a dissatisfied employee against his company, and others. But the criminalization of this game has made it much easier to digitalize the design, organization, and execution of crime and terrorism.

Huge advances are taking place in medical, astrophysical, cognitive, and robotic sciences, to name but a few, thanks to new technologies. However, new forms of crime have also emerged from new technologies and the race for new talents that criminals and terrorists as well as deviant, criminal, failed, and repressive states know how to exploit. These digital geniuses are playing, unfortunately, in a world where the rules of the game are now those of the criminal world. Once introduced, they cannot escape them. This is the case of Ross Ulbricht who, in 2011, thanks to the Internet, completely turned the world drug market upside down. The use of Bitcoin, the invisibility and anonymity of the Dark Web, allowed this brilliant "geek" to suddenly become one of the world's biggest drug traffickers. Identifying himself as a fictional hero (Dread Pirate Roberts from William Goldman's novel *The Princess Bride*), he sold in two years $213 million of illicit products and hacking tools through his online sales site on the Dark Net's "Silk Road".[10] Its appalling and terrifying success

---

[10]Nathan Reiff, article "Who Is Ross Ulbricht, the Dark Net 'Dread Pirate Roberts'?" in Investopedia, (January 15, 2020), https://www.investopedia.com/tech/ross-ulbricht-dark-net-pirate/.

is due, on the one hand, to the genius of an impossible traceability of the origin of the site and its author, and on the other hand, to the organization of the distribution of illicit products to legitimate end-consumers. But it also led him to order the assassination of his potential competitors, which is another dimension of the libertarian game!

Like maritime piracy from ancient times to the present day, computer piracy covets the immense wealth of data flowing along the lines of connection, sailing the oceans formed by the Internet and social networks. There is even a black market in data: a stolen credit card number would be worth up to $15 or a corporate email account would be worth up to $500.[11] Buying 100,000 fake "Followers" on Twitter or 10,000 fake "Likes" on Facebook would cost little more than few hundred US dollars. This is data that is readily available on the hard drive of a laptop or the memory card of a smartphone, either in use or thrown away in e-waste dumps.[12] But fake followers can end up doing damage by hacking, phishing, and infecting against real Twitter followers or Facebook friends with link spam.[13] Just like the mafia hitman, hired geeks or hackers, whether solitary or in cyber-criminal gangs, are on the lookout for any data to be fraudulently exploited.

The physical reality of our identity, our possessions, and our rights can now be reached from the virtual space of the cyber world, elusive to worldly actors and individuals. Criminals and terrorists see this as an opportunity to act from a space beyond the reach of the state and law enforcement agencies. They also become beyond the reach of retaliation from their victims. Legislative, technical, and financial resources are not adapted to these new fields of intervention that crime uses. Cyber-criminals and cyber-terrorists are untouchable, like the astronaut in his satellite who cannot be hit by a soldier's gun. In this sense, cyber-space offers exceptional facilitating conditions for organized crime and terrorism.

In April 2020, nearly 4.57 billion people were active Internet users, representing 59% of the world's population. China, India, and the United

---

[11] Keith Hartwig, Research Paper, "Digital Waste & Cyber-Crime: Examining the Relationship", (December 2016).

[12] *Ibid.*

[13] Megan Marrs, article "Buying Twitter Followers: The (Cheap) Price of Friendship", in Wordstream, (February 25, 2020), https://www.wordstream.com/blog/ws/2013/05/16/buying-twitter-followers-cheap-price-friendship.

States are the countries with the largest number of Internet users.[14] Through the Internet, facilitation takes the form of these fraudulent, intrusive, and non-violent digital actions, without any real physical and human contact or interaction, which help criminals commit theft, cyber-attacks, and hijacking more easily and discreetly. They are also activities where the Internet is used to promote and support terrorist acts on a larger scale, such as propaganda (including recruitment, radicalization, and incitement to terrorism), financing, training, planning, and execution of cyber-attacks.[15] These instruments and methods of facilitation exponentially increase the threats, detrimental effects, and impact of crime on the privacy of individuals in a hyper-connected global world. Cyber-attacks and cybercrimes are committed at the speed of Internet connections and with extreme virality since the effects are immediate, instantaneous, and global in scale. The anonymity offered by cyberspace means that it is impossible to identify and trace the virtual origin of criminal acts and their perpetrators.

Cybercrime continues to grow around the world and is rapidly evolving from an emerging threat to a criminal enterprise with a market value that is now believed to exceed that of the global illicit drug economy.[16] Cybercrime and cyber-terrorism include criminal acts committed through or against computers and telecommunications networks. The computer is both the target and the weapon. Cybercrime includes Botnets,[17] networks of infected computers controlled to send spam and carry out flood attacks or DDoS.[18] Cybercrime also includes "hacking", which allows identity theft to embezzle funds, and fraudulent "phishing" or other social engineering attacks.[19] Particularly aggressive are online extortion for ransom,

---

[14] https://www.statista.com/statistics/617136/digital-population-worldwide/.

[15] UNODC Report 2012, "The Use of Internet for Terrorist Purposes", Eds. United Nations, pp. 3–12.

[16] The value of cybercrime is estimated at $6 trillion while value of counterfeits is $1.3 trillion and value of drug trafficking $650 billion.

[17] Vicky Ngo-lam, article in Information Security Magazine, "Cyber Crime: Types, Examples, and What Your Business Can Do", (December 24, 2019).

[18] DDoS (Distributed Denial of Service) is a malicious attempt to disrupt the normal traffic of a targeted server, service or network by overwhelming the target or its infrastructure with a massive stream of fake Internet traffic.

[19] Phishing is the sending of deceptive messages by e-mail or other channels, leading Internet users to provide personal information, access malicious websites or download malicious payloads.

malware that encrypts data on a local computer and demands a ransom to unlock it. Finally, there are content-related offenses, such as the online distribution of child pornography, but also offenses related to copyright and intellectual property rights. Cybercrime affects all aspects of our lives, be it individual or social, economic, political, or diplomatic.[20]

Cyberspace is now legitimized by information and communication tools and also by the culture of new technologies. It has virtualized the *modus operandi* of information and identity theft, online corruption and intimidation, insider fraud, manipulation of banking, financial, and personal information, as well as fraudulent use of Internet and social networks accounts. It has digitized the illicit trade in goods, people, and capital online from the Dark Web, and also from global social networking platforms (Facebook, Google, eBay, and others). These are the same social networks that, thanks to hacking, make our "Like" our worst enemy by making it one of the main sources of crime penetration in our daily lives;[21] these are the same digital platforms that make "cookies" the spies of our privacy[22] in a society of over-consumption and exacerbated marketing.

Thus, cyberspace has brought about several changes in the very nature of crime.

Cyberspace has given crime and criminals new faces and characteristics. Applications, avatars, disposable devices, and the Dark Web facilitate the concealment of criminal transactions, socialization in subcultures (blogs, fora, etc.), and the networking of people involved in illicit or unconventional behavior. Specialized fora and discussion platforms in cyberspace have created virtual spaces for networking and building reliable underground markets for illicit drugs, weapons, wildlife products, prostitution, slavery, child pornography, and counterfeit goods. Deviant ideological groups may incite terrorism, espionage, or health risks.

---

[20]Loretta J. Stalans and Mary A. Finn (2016), "Understanding How the Internet Facilitates Crime and Deviance", *Victims & Offenders*, Vol. 11(4), 501–508, DOI: 10.1080/15564886.2016.1211404.

[21]P.W Singer and E. Brooking, article "The Real Cyber Threat Is Your "Likes: Weaponization of Social Media", *The Intelligencer*, Vol. 25(1), (Spring-Summer 2019).

[22]According to Kaspersky Labs, cyber-attacks can hijack cookies and, therefore, private browsing sessions. The danger lies in their ability to track individuals' browsing histories. Such "Big Brother" type of behavior can pose a security concern, https://www.kaspersky.com/resource-center/definitions/cookies.

No norms or rules of state governance, through law enforcement or the judiciary, really apply to these covert networks, even though they are not chaotic. Indeed, geographic communities have shifted to online communities of actors hidden behind their anonymity. In an application of the principle of community cohesion, the members of a site or forum seek interactions with others whose levels of deviance and motivation are compatible and similar. A pedophile will not look for images of sexual abuse, for example, in the community of an illegal site selling weapons. The Dark Web is the underground and occult web in which search engines cannot detect sites. It is self-regulating, even though it is much larger than the traditional web, which is regulated and controlled by states and by computer, telecommunications, and social network multinational companies.

Thus, cyberspace has altered the relationship between the criminal and his victim. The physical proximity characteristic of the criminal act has disappeared in cyberspace. Now, through the misuse of computers, the Internet and social networks, the criminal affects mass victims, who are unknown to him (with the exception of cases of defamation, identity theft, or targeted attacks). Viruses, for example, can be widely spread to infect large numbers of indiscriminate victims. The asymmetry between the attacker and his victim, between the means and the results, is a characteristic of cybercrime.[23]

On the other hand, there are "Advanced Persistent Threats" (APTs), which refer to highly planned, sophisticated, and prolonged attacks. They aim to achieve a specific objective, for example, in terms of dismantling infrastructure or obtaining specific information about a person or organization.[24] APTs are usually linked to state-sponsored cyber-attacks, such as Stuxnet and Flame. State-sponsored cyber-attacks, which target the computer networks of another state, are increasingly common. Targets are of course military sites, political or financial institutions, but also businesses, critical civilian infrastructure, and others. The aim is to disrupt the functioning of a territory — its economy, its finances, its political regime and government, or its social stability are completely based on computer

---

[23] Christian Aghroum, « cyberterrorisme et sécurité des entreprises » in Cairn. Info- « Sécurité et stratégie » April 28, 2017, pp. 46–51, https://www.cairn.info/revue-securite-et-strategie-2017-4-page-46.htm.

[24] https://en.wikipedia.org/wiki/Advanced_persistent_threat.

systems and telecommunications networks, whose interruption causes paralysis, collapse, and chaos.[25]

Even if the evidence is lacking, certain states are often blamed for many geopolitical cyber-attacks. The WannaCry attack was allegedly launched by North Korea.[26] Stuxnet is a computer worm discovered in 2010 that was allegedly designed by the NSA (National Security Agency) in the USA in collaboration with a specialized unit of the Israeli army.[27] Moscow has been accused of having created the NotPetya malware, which destroys data on an infected system.[28] On the other hand, cyber-attacks against large companies (hacking into Samsung, iPhone, Google, or Facebook accounts) are more likely to originate in private entities in the USA, China, Japan, or even France.[29] Also, the spread of disinformation has been a global concern since the Russian interferences in the 2016 US elections. Hundreds of fake social media accounts including Facebook, Twitter, and Telegram were found spreading disinformation attempting to influence national discourse in Israel during the 2019 Israeli elections, which might be attributed to Iran, Saudi Arabia, and Russia.[30]

The anonymity provided by cyberspace allows unscrupulous behavior by both cyber offenders and cybercriminals, away from the reproachful gaze of others, insensitive to any social, moral, religious, or ideological inhibitions. It is the liberating, somewhat juvenile and often arrogant feeling of being invisible, elusive, capable of ubiquity, outside the limits of time and space and the constraints of the social contract. As an illustration, during the COVID-19 crisis, online cyber-ransom attacks have been a growing threat since January 2020. Hidden by their anonymity,

---

[25] Information Report No. 681 from the French Senate, about the Cyber Defense, by M. Jean-Marie Bockel, Senator, pp. 7–17.

[26] BBC News "Cyber-attack: US and UK blame North Korea for WannaCry", (December 19, 2017), https://www.bbc.com/news/world-us-canada-42407488.

[27] Ellen Nakashima and Joby Warrick, article "Stuxnet was work of U.S. and Israeli experts, officials say" in Washington Post, (June 2, 2012).

[28] Aparna Banerjea, article "NotPetya: How a Russian malware created the world's worst cyberattack ever" in Business Standard Magazine, (August 27, 2018).

[29] Jennifer Mertens, Article « La France parmi les pays d'où proviennent le plus de cyberattaques », in Le Soir (BE) Newspaper-Geeko, (May 7, 2019), https://geeko.lesoir.be/2019/05/07/la-france-parmi-les-pays-dou-proviennent-le-plus-de-cyberattaques/.

[30] Camille Bigot, Cyber Threat Intelligence Analyst, article in "Manipulation, Disruption & Espionage: The 2019 Israël Elections", *Security Alliance Magazine*, (April 5, 2019).

anonymous hackers abuse and consider as easy prey American hospitals already weakened by the increase in the number of patients and an acute shortage of equipment and resources due to the pandemic.[31] Also, since the beginning of the pandemic, we have seen the looting of health equipment reserves, all kinds of scams on the Internet, the online sale of counterfeit health products or medicines, the explosion of cyber-attacks to hack into data, fake news on social networks that confuse people's minds and take advantage of irrational but all-too human behavior with mixed fears, anxieties, and hopes.

The victim, in turn, doesn't know his executioner…. There's nothing personal in the attack. It is about exploiting the flaws and vulnerability of computer systems in a global society, hyper-connected by the Internet and social networks on which, ultimately, all aspects of our lives depend. Thus, as long as the adversary remains invisible and anonymous, the enemy cannot be defined and responses to cyber-attacks are limited, ineffective, or even non-existent.

Time scales have also evolved in the cyberspace dimension. The time of the crime, the time of the police investigation, and the time of justice are no longer adequate. Cyber-fraud, computer hacking, identity theft, or the manipulation of financial and accounting information are happening at the speed of light. The police can only investigate at the pace of administrative procedures, in accordance with the democratic rule of law, and the state justice system can only charge at the pace of judicial bureaucracy. The virality and anonymity of computer fraud allow the crime and its harmful effects to spread worldwide, almost instantaneously, without any real possibility of determining its origin and, above all, irreversibly. For example, one's reputation and private life can be damaged or even destroyed by cyberstalking, in the time of a click, and with irreparable moral and psychological damage. The fault is committed and its effects spread even before it can be observed and its perpetrators determined.

The globalization of the world economy has also led to a globalization of crime and of the illicit economy. The growth in the volume of world trade is exponential and unprecedented. The process of state building in developing, transitional, and emerging countries (for example, after decolonization in Africa and after the fall of the USSR in Central Asia) is

---

[31] Maggie Miller and Olivia Beavers, article "Hospitals Brace for Increase in Cyberattacks", in The Hill, (April 19, 2020), https://thehill.com/policy/cybersecurity/493410-hospitals-brace-for-increase-in-cyberattacks.

poorly controlled. The volumes of dirty and laundered money circulating in the international financial systems are critical and even indispensable to world order. Banks seize opportunities to access that laundered money to inject it into the global economy and participate in the recovery of the global financial crisis, and thus, in the permanent logic of capitalism.[32] These various factors and opportunities have made states, companies, and individuals vulnerable to the penetration of organized crime and terrorism.

Cyberspace is made up of a multitude of networks. These agile and dynamic building blocks associate and dissociate in different ways according to circumstances and needs. This cyber dimension makes it possible with a local criminal impact to produce effects on a global scale. This is possible, among other things, because of divergent jurisdictions that do not agree on the definition and means of repression to be applied to the phenomenon of cybercrime.[33]

The nature of the Internet further stimulates deviant and criminal activities, as there is no centralized government agency responsible for setting appropriate standards of conduct and enforcing criminal laws in specific countries. In this fragmented legislative environment, conduct that is illegal in some countries is considered legal in other countries. Cyber offenders can then choose to host their websites in the jurisdictions that have the least severe legal consequences. Legislative gaps in the criminalization of cyberspace in any country create havens for offenders, criminals, and terrorists that may affect other countries. These differences in criminalization pose challenges to effective international cooperation in criminal matters against cybercrime.[34] For example, Ross Ulbricht was convicted of seven counts related to the illicit online marketplace Silk Road in the United States and sentenced to life imprisonment. Almost immediately after the closure of the site in 2013, Thomas White, a former site administrator, launched Silk Road 2.0. After one year, Thomas White, also known as "Dread Pirate Roberts 2", doubled the profits of his

---

[32] Bernard Touboul, article "The Role of Money Laundering in International Organised Crime and Terrorism" published in the Winter 2018–19 Edn. Vol. 24(3), of *AFIO's Intelligencer Journal* [US].

[33] Summer Walker, "Cyber Insecurities: A guide to the UN cybercrime debate", Global Initiative Against Transnational Organized Crime, (March 2019).

[34] UNODC Report on "Comprehensive Study on Cybercrime", (February 2013) Chapters 3 and 4.

predecessor. In 2014, on trial in the United Kingdom, he finally pleaded guilty to drug trafficking, money laundering, child pornography, and posting indecent images of children online. He faced five years and four months in prison in the UK jurisdiction. Given the long penalties incurred by Ulbricht in the United States, it seems that White has done well in the UK![35]

Moreover, the criminal activity through cyberspace shows no direct physical violence.[36] Law enforcement agencies focus their efforts and resources on crimes that are considered a priority because of their obvious nature of physical violence or bloodshed, but also because of budgetary constraints and public opinion. Recently, law enforcement agencies have been considering cybercrime facilitation activities as criminal offenses. Indeed, these computer-assisted activities help criminals and terrorists perpetrate their crimes and trafficking that affect the lives and physical and moral integrity of human beings as well as human dignity.

The facilitation of cyberspace results in the organization of new networks for the distribution of illicit goods and services. Online commercial transactions are encrypted by electronic messaging systems such as WhatsApp. They are paid in encrypted currencies such as Bitcoin into virtual online bank accounts. They are routed and delivered by post or express courier with a simple online order. And finally, they are accessible from the Dark Web or from the social network accounts held by the oligopoly of American companies, GAFAM (Google, Amazon, Facebook, Apple, Microsoft), but also the Chinese BATX group of companies (Baidu, Alibaba, Tencent, Xiaomi) and other web and digital giants. Today, these companies control the Tech-Industry market with very large user accounts, data bases, and enormous capacities for innovation in information and communication technologies to the point of creating the notion of a digital-industrial complex.[37] For example, Facebook, accessible from accounts domiciled in Syria, Libya, or Iraq, hosts vast bazaars of weapons online, offering items ranging from handguns and grenades to

---

[35] https://www.techdirt.com/articles/20190412/13210041993/creator-silk-road-20-did-double-business-sentenced-to-only-five-years-prison.shtml.

[36] Earl Moulton, "The Future of Cyber Crime" (2010), https://sciences.ucf.edu/fwg/wp-content/uploads/sites/157/2016/11/MoultonV5.pdf.

[37] Digital-industrial complex relates to the trading of digital data between a few major players in the tech industry, which are increasingly seen as hostile to privacy. This notion recalls what the growing threat of the military-industrial complex was in 1961 in the USA.

heavy machine guns and guided missiles.[38] Following a BBC investigation, Google, Apple, Facebook, and Amazon (GAFA) have been accused
of facilitating illegal slave markets through their applications, particularly
in Kuwait, where there are many domestic maids from Africa.[39] Without
checking the suppliers who sell on its site, the Chinese giant Alibaba is
regularly accused of facilitating fraudsters and distributors of counterfeit
products.[40]

The effective democratization of the Internet and social networks, in
the name of freedom of expression and enterprise, is concomitant with the
democratization of cybercrime. Everyone, computer expert or amateur,
can easily create their own commercial website and business selling illicit
goods and services on the web and the Dark Web. The possible use of
information and communication technologies by a lone wolf terrorist is a
real threat, even if since 9/11 it is still hypothetical since no murderous
terror cyber-attack has officially taken place since then. But the immense
opportunities for users worldwide to buy and sell drugs, weapons, sexually exploited or enslaved children and adults, false passports or other
forged documents, hacking tools (TOR, Trojan Black shade, Spyware,
Ransomware) using digital currencies as a means of payment, is now a
reality.[41,42]

Finally, cyberspace is certainly borderless since data are transferred in
continuous flows beyond the territorial limits of sovereign states. But the
facilities and equipment for transmitting and receiving these flows remain
physical and material. These are the submarine telecommunications
cables, communication satellites, computer equipment, and associated

---

[38] C. J. Chivers in *The NY Times* "Facebook Groups Act as Weapons Bazaars for Militias",
(April 6, 2016).

[39] Darren Boyle, article in DailyMail.co.uk, 'Tech giants including Instagram and Google
are hosting online slave markets where domestic workers are being bought and sold for
less than £3,000 through apps', January 01, 2019, https://www.dailymail.co.uk/news/
article-7640673/Online-slave-markets-use-tech-giants-sell-domestic-staff-Kuwait.html.

[40] Jacob Pramuk and Christina Wilkie, article "Trump Puts Amazon, Alibaba on Notice for Sale
of Counterfeit Goods", CBNC News, (April 3, 2019). Also, *Bloomberg*, (May 6, 2015),
"Nuclear Smugglers Abusing Alibaba Listings Challenge Iran Deal", http://www.bloomberg.
com/news/articles/2015-05-05/nuclear-smugglers-abusing-alibaba-listings-challenge-iran-deal.

[41] Stephen Cobb, article "Next Generation Dark Markets? Think Amazon or eBay for
criminals: The "evolution" of these markets is making cybercrime easier than ever before"
in Welivesecurity.com (December 10, 2018).

[42] Xavier Raufer, "Cyber-Criminologie", Ed. CNRS, pp. 120–125.

electronic devices which depend on investment and financial mobilization by either states or private companies. For example, the communication satellites that enabled the Internet broadcasting of ISIS messages and communication campaigns are manufactured, marketed, and made available to terrorists by European companies[43] (to eventually target terrorist attacks in Europe, by the way!).

In this way, traditional crime is projected into cyberspace. It finds there the tools of facilitation that give it a new dimension with mass effects, more effective, discreet, anonymous, and more immediate. Each scientific innovation (IoT, Artificial Intelligence) systematically becomes a catalyst for all forms of trafficking, traditional crime, and terrorism.

For example, like traditional bank robberies, cyberspace provides the means to rob banks on a large scale for the profit of criminals or the financing of illicit or even terrorist actions.

Case Study: Carbanak

An unprecedented cyber bank robbery recently targeted banking systems and other financial institutions around the world was performed by the Carbanak cyber gang.[44] An international gang of cybercriminals from Russia, Ukraine, and China, Carbanak has attacked more than 100 financial institutions in some 30 countries including Russia, the United States, Germany, Australia, Switzerland, and others. Up to $1 billion was stolen in about two years. Criminals have seized these huge sums of money by hacking by using APT into banks, stealing $8 to $12 million in each raid. The cybercriminals used malicious software to infect the banks' network, allowing them to access employees' computers and thus everything that was happening on the screens of the staff in charge of the money transfer systems. In general, the attackers did not even need to hack into the banks' services once they had entered the network. When it was time to cash in

---

[43] Nicolai Kwasniewski, "How Islamic State Takes Its Terror to the Web", Der Spiegel International on 04/12/2015 — the article explains that "Islamic State is a master at using the Internet to spread propaganda. SPIEGEL ONLINE research indicates European companies (Eutelsat, SES) may be providing the terrorist organization Internet access by satellite dish".

[44] Kaspersky Lab report on "Carbanak APT: The Great Bank Robbery", (February 2015), https://media.kasperskycontenthub.com/wp-content/uploads/sites/43/2018/03/08064518/Carbanak_APT_eng.pdf.

on their activities, the fraudsters used online banking or international payment systems to transfer money to their accounts. Sometimes the stolen money was deposited in banks in China or America. And in other cases, cybercriminals have penetrated into the heart of the banks' accounting systems by inflating the balances of certain accounts before pocketing the extra funds through a fraudulent transaction. For example, take a $1,000 account; the criminals modify it to register $10,000 and then transfer $9,000 to themselves. The account holder doesn't notice anything since the original $1,000 is still there. In addition, the cyber thieves had taken remote control of the banks' ATM and ordered the money to be distributed at a predetermined time, where an accomplice is in position to withdraw the misappropriated funds.

In another area of cybercrime, social networks and online classified ad sites are used by traffickers to market, recruit, sell, and exploit human beings for criminal purposes such as prostitution, child pornography, exploitation, and sexual slavery. Traffickers view human beings as commodities, objects that are exploited and sold for profit. The Internet is massively used by sex traffickers to advertise the sexual services of victims[45] in now known patterns of operation: (1) online classified ad sites are used to post victim ads, and (2) social networking sites are used to recruit victims.

The role of social networking sites and online classified ads on the traditional web has become central in facilitating human trafficking. These classified ad sites such as Craigslist, Backpage in the USA[46] offer sections devoted to employment, housing, sales, discussion forums but also "adult" (or erotic) services and are used to perpetrate human trafficking, sex, and pedophilia.[47] It is also the use made of advertising space on Facebook, Google, and Twitter, for example.[48] While the traditional channels of prostitution, pedophilia, and modern slavery remain in place, online technologies give traffickers unprecedented opportunities to

---

[45] Mark Latonero, *et al.*, Research Report on "Human Trafficking Online: The Role of Social Networking Sites and Online Classifieds", USC Annenberg Center on Communication Leadership & Policy, (September 2011).

[46] Sarah N. Lynch, Lisa Lambert, article "Sex ads website Backpage shut down by U.S. authorities", *Reuters U.S. Legal News*, (April 6, 2018).

[47] See footnote 45.

[48] *Ibid.*

exploit more victims and make their services known across geographical borders. Cyber child pornography is an increasingly visible problem in society today. With the growth in home Personal Computer usage and more readily available access to the web over the past decade, child pornographers have found a convenient venue for sharing child sexual abuse material and horrific pictures of children being sexually abused. Because of the ease of transportation and global communications via the Internet and social networks that can reach deep into villages with promises and images of what a better life could be, many more human beings are being exploited than ever before.[49]

Organized crime syndicates and terrorist organizations operate according to strict rational principles aimed at minimizing risk and maximizing profit. The facilitation provided by cyberspace accelerates the creation of an environment where existing laws are simply disregarded or ignored. The prerogatives that new technologies allow for private purposes are seen not only as justified, but also as an indicator of power.

Being a cybercriminal involves nothing more than downloading software from the Dark Net anonymously, following a procedure available on YouTube, to hack into a Facebook account, buying Bitcoin from a virtual bank account accessible on the web and others. Anyone can be a cybercriminal. And this is one of the main reasons for the inability of law enforcement to profile cybercriminals or cyber terrorists.[50] Anyone can learn quickly, independently, and without a mentor, with little evidence of deviant or fraudulent behavior.[51] Even the most inexperienced hacker finds satisfaction, attraction, and pleasure in his or her activities. Evidence left at the scene of the crime does not exist in a cyberspace without real geography and where the duality of time (past/future) no longer exists.

The life of criminals is simply easier since the risks (of repression or competition) are lower and the profits (from more opportunities and mass victims) much higher. This new environment attracts the less scrupulous,

---

[49] https://highline.huffingtonpost.com/articles/en/the-21st-century-gold-rush-refugees/#/niger.

[50] Jake Moor, article in Welivesecurity, "What Makes a Cybercriminal? Forget Balaclavas or Hoodies; These Cybercriminals are Hiding in Plain Sight", (January 15, 2019).

[51] Stephen Cobb, article "Next Generation Dark Markets? Think Amazon or eBay for criminals: The "evolution" of these markets is making cybercrime easier than ever before", Welivesecurity.com, (December 10, 2018).

facilitates the establishment and development of local and transnational criminal networks, and promotes a cultural model in which money can buy everything, including impunity, political power, social status, and respectability.

The enormous corruptive power of illicit money, coupled with the internal structural weaknesses of states, endangers the very foundations of fragile democratic institutions. Criminals and terrorists are present on a daily basis in the lives of citizens, institutions, and states. They represent the privileged authority to which citizens in distress, deprived of the services of the undermined state evading its most fundamental responsibilities and prerogatives, turn. As an example, due to the COVID-19 crisis, people have lost jobs, daily earning has vanished for many, and the Italian mafia, providing its own loans or cash handouts, is seen as the most realistic option.[52] Already, organized crime and terrorism make up for the inadequacies of the state in terms of social, employment, education, and health in both developing and developed countries. As an example, the Taliban of Afghanistan have quarantined people, imposed curfews and confinement because of COVID-19 in the place of the state, and in a more efficient way![53]

Going forward, the redistribution of governance power between the governments and non-state actors including criminals and terrorists gives the latter a growing role thanks to the vacuum left by the state, which is particularly absent from the governance of cyberspace and Internet. This is one of the key factors of the facilitation of crime and terrorism to which technologies, the Internet, and social networks increasingly contribute.

---

[52] Kevin Sieff, Susannah George and Kareem Fahim, Article "Now Joining the Fight Against Coronavirus: The World's Armed Rebels, Drug Cartels and Gangs", *Washington Post*, (April 14, 2020).

[53] *Ibid.*

https://doi.org/10.1142/9789811229138_0007

Chapter 7

Conclusions and Recommendations

Norman A. Bailey and Bernard Touboul

The principles outlined in the Introduction and the following chapters and case studies illustrate two phenomena that taken together illuminate a reality that deserves much greater attention if it is to be successfully addressed.

Today's reality is that a very significant portion of the world's economic and financial activity is now controlled by criminal syndicates, often allied with terrorist organizations looking to finance their nefarious activities. This phenomenon is manifestly dangerous to the survival of our Western Civilization. Yet, it has now become so embedded in our institutions and their operations that to many people it is simply easier (and safer) to treat it as an integral part of modern social reality, concentrating our attention, time, and resources on the other dangerous elements of the contemporary world, such as Iran or North Korea (which are themselves state facilitators of the criminal/terrorist networks).

All efforts to deal with, much less to defeat, this burgeoning criminal/terrorist network have been a manifest failure. For every gang and terrorist group that is broken up, two or three more emerge. The FARC, the Red Brigades, and the Provisional IRA are no more, but like the proverbial cat and its nine lives, out of the ashes successors or the remnants of the original organizations, such as ISIS and Al Qaeda, are reformed into new terror or criminal organizations. In the meantime, criminal syndicates proliferate and prosper, get richer, buy more facilitators, and corrupt more public officials. At the same time, it is more and more difficult for law-enforcement agencies to apprehend them and for the judicial system to prosecute them.

As we have seen, entire countries are now run like criminal enterprises. Lebanon is now simply an umbrella name under which the terrorist organization Hezbollah grows and spreads out. Guinea-Bissau is the principal West African conduit through which cocaine flows to Europe. Venezuela is considered a narco-state by the US. But they and others are still welcomed in international organizations as if they behaved like other normal countries. There are also the fragile and failed national states that no longer fulfill their responsibilities under their social contracts with their populations; independent justice is non-existent; law enforcement has been replaced by a survival attitude, there is recourse to armed self-defense or to protection by the criminal gangs themselves. There are the "deviant" countries like Russia, Iran, North Korea, and Turkey where they use criminals and terrorists and their facilitators as proxies to covertly undermine Western society and civilization.

In short, this danger is real and immediate — but the measures taken thus far to confront the phenomenon have been seriously flawed and thus largely ineffective.

Until now, most of the anti-criminal/terrorist actions taken by law-enforcement agencies and authorities have been designed to confront them frontally. Given the pervasive infiltration of those same agencies and authorities by the very organizations they are attacking, it is hardly surprising that they are usually ineffective — in other words, the will to succeed is lacking, and in some cases, where corruption is pervasive, entirely absent. And then there are the political calculations: are the direct and indirect costs of fighting crime and terrorism worth the benefits? Is a tolerable status quo not a safer choice especially when crime and terror are political instruments for gaining and maintaining power through the use of proxy violent organizations?

Facilitation for committing crime has never been so evident. Still rarely considered as a crime itself, except for money laundering, facilitation has been even further accelerated and intensified with the advent of the Internet, social networks, and new technologies. The limited results of the struggle against crime and terrorism by the law enforcement agencies and judiciary are eloquent. The risk for a criminal or a terrorist being caught is very small in a disorganized International Community presenting such divergent national criminalization policies for money laundering, terrorism, cybercrime, people trafficking, and so on.

The various chapters of this book suggest the need for a different approach in looking at the causes, the role, and the perspectives of organized crime and terrorism; an interdisciplinary approach for changing the current paradigm, ignoring the reality that the role of crime and terror have become the norm in all aspects of billions of people's daily lives.

Financial, social, political, economic, health, and other crises and challenges have highlighted the limits of many countries' competencies and capacities in effectively dealing with the issues. Poor governmental and administrative capacity represents an open gate to the penetration and facilitation of organized crime and terrorism. It is regrettable that through their politicians' declarations (especially in Europe), some societies are taught that they should learn how to live with crime and terrorism, and implicitly learn to tolerate the existence and the role of crime and terror in their lives.

However, the facilitators of criminal and terrorist organizations and of their activities should be pursued and prosecuted as much as the criminals that they help, and above all exposed. This power of dissuasion is a prerogative that nation-states should retrieve. Lawyers, accountants, public relations specialists, consultants, and other professionals; businesses in all fields of activity; banks and other financial organizations, and NGOs which aid and assist, finance and enable the criminal/terrorist networks in their nefarious activities must be identified and exposed publicly as well as prosecuted.

Facilitators of all sorts are jealous of their reputations, and exposure and shaming will thus be effective at least to sully their image and adversely affect their clientele.

It may be objected that this approach will also be impeded by the fact that the competent authorities as well as the media are extensively infiltrated by the network. To some extent that is undoubtedly true. The trust of the citizenry in their countries' representatives, institutions, and associated elites have vanished in much of the world.

Therefore, raising the awareness of the citizenry on the real world rulers' intentions, explaining the responsibility of consumers in a globalized world that marketers shape with their media manipulations are essential building-blocks to at least limit (even if it is too late to eradicate) the current normalization of crime and terror in states, institutions, enterprises, and people's lives. Encouraging transparency of information, the integrity-based legitimacy of state, and the participation of citizens in influential social organizations (political parties, NGOs, businesses, and civil society generally) should be key principles of governance for preventing facilitators from helping criminals and terrorists reach their objectives.

In our contemporary, increasingly complex and global world, we constantly see situations such as: "Law and accounting firms a and b set up front companies for drug syndicates x and y; public relations and consulting firms c and d whitewashed the activities of terrorist groups m and n; oil marketing firms f and g bought ISIS oil at a discount from ISIS and sold it into the market; Deutsche Bank or Den Danske Bank through their branches in o and p financed syndicates q and r which are allied to terrorist groups s and t, which are sponsored by deviant or compliant states u and v".

But complexity is not synonymous with chaos. All people and organizations have their rational motivations and *modus operandi*, search for satisfaction and pleasure, and have a need for being identified and recognized as unique. Therefore, a strategy of naming, shaming, and sanctioning, supported by strong measures for raising public consciousness and reinforcing the structure of governance at national, regional, and international levels can be decisive.

Necessary corrective measures will involve legislation specifically directed to target the facilitators as well as specialized units in law enforcement agencies tasked with identifying and prosecuting them. Such steps will need to be well financed but that should be no problem as terminating programs that are clearly not working should free up plentiful resources.

The day this starts to happen is the same day that the massive threat to Western society — its economic, political, social, moral, and ethical structure — from the criminal/terrorist networks will begin to recede.

And that would not be a moment too soon.

Bibliographical Note

For further reading on the subject of the facilitators of Criminal and Terrorist networks, besides some of the sources referred to in the text, we recommend the following works:

- Louise I Shelley, *Dark Commerce: How A New Illicit Economy Is Threatening Our Future*, Princeton, NJ, Princeton University Press, 2018.
- Michael Miklausik and Jacqueline Brewer, eds., *Convergence: Illicit Networks and National Security in the Age of Globalization*, Washington, D.C., National Defense University Press, 2013.
- John A. Cassara, *Trade-Based Money Laundering: The Next Frontier in International Money Laundering Enforcement*, John Wiley & Sons, Inc., Hoboken, New Jersey, 2016.
- Jean-François Gayraud, *Théorie des Hybrides. Terrorisme et crime organisé*, CNRS Éditions, 2011.
- Jean-François Gayraud, *Le Monde des mafias: Géopolitique du crime organisé*, Ed. Odile Jacob, 2008.
- Nicolas Henin, *Jihad Academy: Nos erreurs face à l'Etat islamique*, Fayard, 2015.

Index

A

Advanced Persistent Threats (APTs), 75, 81
Al Qaeda business model in Afghanistan, 47–48
AML/TF Transaction Monitoring systems, 26
artificial intelligence-based technologies, 1, 15, 18, 83

B

BATX (Baidu, Alibaba, Tencent, Xiaomi), 79
Bitcoin, use of, 31, 71, 79, 83
Black Market Peso Exchange (BMPE), 34
block-chain-based crypto-money, 44
blue-collar criminals, 19
Botnets, 73
The Bubble of American Supremacy, 60
business facilitators
    Al Qaeda business model in Afghanistan, 47–48
    business strategies and practices, 41
    coexistence, 49

corporate strategy, 44
criminal investment in legal enterprises, 39–40, 45
economic model phenomena, 46–47
European agricultural subsidy mechanisms, 45
Global Financial Integrity, 46
influence of criminal and terrorist business, 48–49
ISIS Inc, 42–43, 48
Italian or Russian mafias, 46
jihadism (see also jihadism (case study)), 49–51
legal businesses and illegal activities, 39, 41, 44–45, 50
oil companies in ISIS territory, control of, 42–43
reverse money laundering, 3, 43
risk-assessment, 40
sectors with criminal involvement, 45
strategies to combat crime/ terrorism, 40
tax havens, fraud schemes, 42–43

www.ingramcontent.com/pod-product-compliance
Lightning Source LLC
Chambersburg PA
CBHW071941260326
41914CB00004B/710